THE CREATIVE WRITER'S TOOLKIT

Mastering the Art of Consistency

by

Vanessa McKay

.

ABOUT THE AUTHOR

Vanessa McKay is an author, editor, publisher, coach and creative writing instructor based in Kwinana, Western Australia. Her journey as a writer began in childhood, fuelled by a deep-seated need to make sense of her world and find her voice. Through years of perseverance, self-discovery and honing her craft, Vanessa has emerged as a contemporary fiction author with four published novels and more to come.

Drawing from her rich life experiences and the challenges she's overcome, Vanessa now dedicates herself to nurturing other writers' creative spirits. She conducts engaging workshops, creating supportive environments where aspiring authors can explore their potential and develop their unique voices.

Vanessa's teaching philosophy emphasises the importance of a regular writing practice, embracing one's authentic self, and the power of persistence in the face of self-doubt.

In addition to her local and online classes, Vanessa hosts immersive creative writing retreats, offering writers the opportunity to deeply engage with their craft in inspiring settings. These retreats combine focused writing time with guided exercises, group discussions and one-on-one mentoring sessions.

With a warm, encouraging approach and a wealth of personal insights, Vanessa is dedicated to empowering writers at all stages of their journey, helping them to unlock their creativity and share their stories with the world.

First Edition
ISBN: 978-0-6458851-8-7 (paperback)
ISBN: 978-0-6458851-9-4 (ebook)

Published in Australia by Tea Time Press

TEA TIME PRESS
INDEPENDENT BOOK PUBLISHER

Dedicated to my family.
Thank you for all the notebooks, pens, teacups
and candles you have gifted me.
I have loved them all.

CONTENTS

THE
CREATIVE WRITER'S
TOOLKIT

'The privilege of a lifetime is to become who you truly are.'

Carl Jung

Writing Practice: a consistent, dedicated routine of putting words on the page, regardless of quality or outcome, with the aim of developing one's writing skills, exploring creativity, and nurturing the habit of writing. It involves regular, often timed, writing exercises that encourage free expression without judgement, helping writers overcome self-doubt, find their voice and build confidence in their craft. Writing practice is not about producing polished work, but rather about engaging with the process of writing itself as a means of growth and self-discovery.

Rules for Writing Practice

There are writing exercises throughout this book that will form the beginnings of your writing practice – please keep in mind the following as you proceed through this book.

- Keep your hand moving
- No editing—don't worry about grammar and spelling
- No crossing out
- No stopping
- Dig deep, don't shy away from what comes
- Give it all

WHAT IS WRITING?

'We write to taste life twice,
in the moment and in retrospect.'

Anais Nin

Writing is so much more than just putting words on a page. It's a journey of self-discovery, a tool for change, and a bridge between minds.

Through writing you can:

Share your voice: writing gives you the power to share your unique perspective with the world. It's your personal megaphone, amplifying your thoughts and ideas.

Paint with words: through creative writing, you can craft entire worlds, breathe life into characters, and weave tales that captivate hearts and minds. Your imagination is the only limit!

Preserve moments in time: writing allows you to capture fleeting thoughts, preserve precious memories, and document history as it unfolds. It's like creating a time capsule with words.

Inspire and persuade: with the right words, you can move mountains (or at least people's opinions). Writing is a powerful tool for advocacy, persuasion and inspiring change.

Explore the depths of your mind: writing is like going on an adventure inside your own head. It helps you untangle complex thoughts, develop new ideas, and see things from different angles. You might just discover things about yourself you never knew. It's a journey of personal growth and self-discovery.

Heal and grow: sometimes, the best therapist is a blank page. Writing can be a soothing balm for the soul, helping you process emotions and experiences.

Open doors: in many careers, the pen (or keyboard) is mightier than the sword. Strong writing skills can be your ticket to professional success.

Entertain: from side-splitting comedies to heart-wrenching dramas, writing has the power to take readers on emotional roller coasters and leave them wanting more.

Writing
Exercise

Take out your notebook and pen. Set your timer for ten minutes or set your intention to write for three pages. Describe a moment in your life that changed you. First, write about it as you experienced it in real time. Then write about the same moment from your current perspective, reflecting on how it shaped you.

How does writing about this experience in these two different ways affect your understanding of it?

WHY WRITE?

'I write because there is a voice within me
that will not be stilled.'

Sylvia Plath

I write to make sense of my world. I have done this since early childhood. I was adopted at six months and have forever felt on the outside of society. I see things, I remember things and as a child, my voice was silenced. It is a practice I have continued into my adulthood. Outwardly, I am a closed book. I write contemporary fiction and after filling a stack of notebooks, writing six unpublished manuscripts, and four published books, I have found my voice.

In person, I have little to say, but I will write mountains. I will write until the end of my days. I write because I have too much to say, because I was silenced, because I was told to be quiet, because I was told I was wrong, that my opinions didn't matter, and by extension that I didn't matter. So, I write. I write to remember a childhood that no one else is around to remember. I write to understand how I feel. I write to be heard. By someone. It is easy to see who I am and the things that I have gone through by reading my books. The trouble with that is the part that is me is mixed up with so much that isn't. We know fiction books are not an accurate depiction of the author, but we are in there hidden somewhere between the lines.

I have filled notebook after notebook with my random thoughts and my meanderings. I always intended to write a story or be creative, but for many years it all came back to me and whatever sadness, anger or disappointment I was carrying around. This wasn't writing. This was journalling and much of this writing has gone and has been destroyed.

I write to understand my mind, to prevent myself from going crazy, to feel like I have had my say, to practise communication, to live many times, to not waste my life, to share, to resonate, to be. I think that is it. To be, I actually don't care if anyone I know reads my work. However, I care right now that you are reading my work. I care that I have taken the time to write this work, to refine it, to work with my editors and to share with you that I am a writer.

Natalie Goldberg says, 'Don't be tossed away,' stay true to your writer self and know that it is so much more than a passing phase left over from school. It is in your bones, it is deep within your psyche, it is an itch without satisfaction, you are a writer and so you must write!

Not everyone feels this, or maybe I should say not everyone is possessed by this need, this unending drive, this want, this calling. It is so personal and so innate that we often feel guilty taking time away from our daily responsibilities. We have to squirrel away our writing time, settling for staying up late at night, waking up extra early, sneaking it in at kids' sports events because you might be asked:

- What are you doing?
- What are you writing about?
- Are you writing about me?
- You think you're a writer?

The truth is that if you don't hit it out of the ballpark relatively quickly and become a success, then what are you doing? You and I both know that you can't spend your life living a pipe dream. Smoke doesn't pay the bills! So I get a job; I have tried on many careers thinking it is best to just find something that makes a dollar. Writing, after all, is nothing but a self-indulgence. No one ever makes it, not really. Success in writing is reserved for the likes of Margaret Atwood, Stephen King, Jodi Picoult and other greats, far removed from my realm of ability.

BUT …

The world is full of writers we have never heard of who have made it well enough for writing to be their world. I want you to write this down. **Persistence is the only difference between those who make it and those who fall by the wayside.** Faced with all the objections and criticism from those they love, they persisted. And you should too.

I have been many things in my money-earning career, but one thing was always constant: my pen and my notebook. I tried to leverage a minor income on writing sites, sold copy for magazines and websites, wrote for sports clubs, wrote my books, blog posts, ad copy, newsletters—anything, anywhere, just for the joy of writing. I have six partially edited novels on my hard drive and four books published. I make little money from any of them, but they are there and even at my age, it is just the beginning.

I laugh at that last sentence: just the beginning. I have written millions of words over the years, I have opened my mind, got past the dribble, the writing that says I am having a bad day, my husband doesn't love me, my children don't listen, nobody cares about me so I am just going to go home and eat worms. Clear out the clutter, the mind is full of it. The poor me, the if only, that has to be honoured, and it has to be set free. Under that, under everyday colossal pointless words that describe our shallow existence, is the gold. Dig in, write and write, Natalie Goldberg will tell you to give yourself permission to write the worst junk ever. Get rid of it. Clear the cupboard and be prepared to display the good stuff, it is under there, under the mess, and it is beautiful. Don't let anybody tell you it is a waste of time or money. If you write, you are a writer, that is it. You may spend your days working on other things to pay the bills, but while you do that you are viewing the world with the heart of a writer, and nothing can stop you. You only have this life. Do what you are meant to do. Write stories, even if no one around you is keen to read them. Write. For the time being, write for no other reason other than you want to. That is reason enough. Like meeting a friend for coffee, washing the car, doing the gardening, watching a movie, breathing, eating and loving. You are a writer. You must write.

'It is never too late to be what you might have been.'

Mary Ann Evans

Write with no expectations of paying the bills. Write with no expectations that you will write a great novel and be famous and maybe Netflix will pick up your manuscript. Sure, all that can happen. If you work hard enough, and get lucky enough, why not? But for now, I ask you to just write for the sake of writing. Anything, any gibberish, refuse nothing that urges your pen to move. We are not seeking perfection; we are practising our craft. We are writing words, rolling them around the page, building an understanding of ourselves and the world around us, our place in it, your job as a writer, an observer, a storyteller. Write.

My husband asked me one day why I need to write. We had been together nearly twenty years at this time, and this was the first time he had asked. I think it had finally become obvious to him I wasn't ever going to stop, that writing was as much a part of me as putting on my shoes. I always had a notebook in my bag that I only use for writing practice. I have pens everywhere and at least half a dozen in my bag anytime I go out. I read books on craft, fan girl over my favourite authors, google my mentors, soak up their words of encouragement, try my best to be a writer. No matter what fills my day, I soak up the words of other writers. I told him that if I didn't write, I would go crazy. I joked that the voices inside my head wouldn't shut up and had to get out. I have to write. That is all there is to it.

Writing
Exercise

Take out your notebook. Somewhere in the back of your notebook, begin a list of story ideas.

THE CATERMAN

'You have to write the book that wants to be written.
And if the book will be too difficult for grown-ups,
then you write it for children.'

Madeleine L'Engle

I remember my first time. My first creative writing experience. I was in grade two; the class was tasked with drawing a picture. I made a caterpillar, bright, colourful and easy to shape. Our teacher, Mrs Reinboth, sliced our artwork in half with a guillotine as twenty-something astonished six-year-olds looked on. She then stacked the pictures into two piles. We each waited for our name to be called and were given the top half of our picture and told to take the next picture from the pile of bottoms. Confused, we did as we were told and returned to our seats with a picture in each hand.

We were to create a new picture by sticking both images on to a fresh sheet of paper. The chatter broke out. This sounded like something good. Glue pots were unleashed and new images were created and shared with our desk neighbours.

But that wasn't the best bit. Next we had to write a poem about the new image. A poem. I couldn't believe it. I was going to get to write a poem, and we had the entire afternoon to do it. Words, a poem; words, my own words. My teacher even said we would all be writers for the day.

There I sat, six-year-old me, staring at my picture. Half caterpillar, half man. I remember the poem to this day:

> A caterman is funny
> Because he walks half on his tummy
> When he tries to sit down
> He lays half on the ground
> And sits there like a stuffed dummy.

I was so proud of that poem and the way it just poured out of me. Even if my teacher appeared a little underwhelmed when I read it to her. She didn't like the part about the stuffed dummy. Critic. No accounting for taste.

It was this exercise that changed me from a child who simply made up stories and play acts to being a writer. I fell in love with books, story time and learning how to write. As my writing skills grew so did my stories. My stories reflected my experiences and became my counsel. My writing saw me through some turbulent times in my childhood.

Writing
Exercise

Take out your notebook and pen.

On the top of your page, write—I am a writer because …

If you get stuck for what comes next, rewrite the prompt—I am a writer because … and keep going for ten minutes, no stopping.

EXPLORING THE
CREATIVE WOUND

'There is no greater agony
than bearing an untold story inside you.'

Maya Angelou

As a heartsick teenager searching for love and acceptance, I fell hard for a boy. It was love, at least that is what it felt like. It was an emotional roller coaster, and I wrote stream after stream of poetry about how much I loved him and how fast I would die if we broke up. This was all recorded in an unused A4 schoolbook, I would push deep under my mattress before leaving the house.

Jean, my adopted mum, had her friend Iris over for tea, who just happened to be my boyfriend's mum. He had told her about the poetry I wrote for him, and she thought it was lovely that someone loved her boy so. How cute and smitten we were.

Tired of being left out of my loop, Jean tore my room apart until she found it. Together, the two mothers sat reading my words, not meant for them. While Iris said how clever I was, Jean said—she didn't write this, how could she?

I returned home to find them both sitting in the lounge of the rented house on Lewington Street in Rockingham we had moved into temporarily after our arrival from Adelaide. It had come furnished with relics from the 1970s. My book sat on the Formica coffee table between them. I raced to grab it. My face was hot. *Had they read this?*

Iris told me I was very talented and for a moment my embarrassment turned to pride. Then she excused herself, thanking Jean for the tea. We walked her to her car in the drive and waved her off. I still held my book in my hand as I followed Jean up the stone steps into the house. In the narrow hallway, she turned and ripped the book from my hands and walked through to the lounge room. I wasn't sure what was going on but I knew the feeling in the pit of my stomach, that gripping, then the heat that would rise to my face while a chill ran through my bones.

'Plagiarism is against the law. You copied these, you can't go around pretending this is your work. How could you write something like this? Admit it you didn't write this, you are no writer.'

It was winter. The old house had a stone fireplace, and it was roaring when she threw it in the flames. Despite my protests, she insisted I was lying and that I would be found out. I could go to jail. I knew her, and I knew that regardless of what I said, the book would burn and she would never believe me. It didn't matter, I didn't write for her. She would often accuse me of lying when I produced something beyond what she thought I was capable of or that she couldn't comprehend.

My love poems were on fire. This was 1985 and there were no copies, no internet, no Microsoft Word for soft copies. I stomped to my room, slammed the door hard enough to shake the window frame, found another book, and started writing as much as I could from memory. As hard as I tried, I couldn't capture the feeling, I couldn't get it right. I could write new poetry but the original feeling was lost. All I could feel through my tears and determination was sadness and disappointment at her attitude. I felt guilty, too. What if I had somehow copied these poems from someone else, but who? I had only read a few poems outside of school assignments. Besides their emotional tone and rhyming structure, I doubt they can be considered anything beyond free-form poetry. I had no idea. How could I know? I was fourteen years old, our house had no books, and I hadn't even heard of the internet.

Looking back, even as a child, I was reluctant to show my work to my parents. I have an early memory of writing my name for the first time—V A N E S S A—when I must have been four years old, and Jean saying, 'That is too good, there is no way you could have written that.' She handed me the pen and told me to write my name again, to prove it was me. I was horrified. My young brain could not perceive that she was playing a game. She thought she was being funny, winding me up. I just cried. *'I did do it. Why don't you believe me?'* I realise that the whole relationship with my adoptive mother goes deeper than what I am about to unpack now. Adopted or not, she was my primary caregiver. But here it is, this is where my skin was first scratched. Only to be dug deeper and deeper as I grew. She kept twisting her knife into the wound until I finally went no contact in my mid-twenties.

I walked around with this festering wound, the one that said I couldn't do it, I couldn't go to university, I couldn't be a writer, she criticised everything I did. She told me I had always been wrong, and that is why my mother didn't want me. Everything about me was wrong. I had teachers tell me otherwise and I would get excited and try to heal the wound with the band-aids they gave me.

Later, I would confidently stride into writing workshop after workshop and say, I am a writer. I would pull out my pen, my notebook, push down my anxiety enough to stay in the room but never enough to read out loud, but I would keep going. I kept turning up. It is a club if you will that I desperately wanted to belong to, and where I have come to learn that my quirks and social anxiety are shared with the majority, who practise putting on a face and pretending for the time being that maybe we have something worthwhile to say.

I haven't healed the wound. I hold on to everything negative that has ever been said about my writing, even from my editor. (Yes, I know that is their job. I am an editor and I know sometimes you just have to tell the author that something they've written is wrong). I hold on to the days when my books don't sell, finding a typo, every negative thing that can happen when you release a book, but I do something else as well. I keep the positive. I print it off and stick it in my journal—I don't keep the negatives. They spin around my head rent-free, all the way back to my childhood.

Honestly, I don't know if the creative wound can be healed. It goes on to varying degrees of sepsis to feed my imposter syndrome. The only way forward is to keep going. Write, own your writing, own your time and your ability to put one word in front of another; don't, as Natalie Goldberg would say, 'be tossed away.' Write that quote in your notebook, write it on your wall. If you are driven to put pen to paper, know that it is so much more than self-indulgence.

I have been practising karate for nearly twenty years and I will never be an Olympian or world champion, and none of it matters. I don't have to be the best. I just have to do my best. I expect nothing from karate, except maybe I would have a better chance at defending myself than if I had never done karate. But it's okay. I keep putting my plus-size arse in my karate gi once or twice a week and train. How many things do we do in our lives without expecting to be the best and without any other pay-off beyond the act itself? Think about all the activities that you do without being the best at them and without receiving any accolades—you drive without winning races, you clean, you cook, you go to the gym—go ahead and write them all down. How long is your list? Get down to the nitty-gritty. I water the lawn without winning best garden in the street, I walk the block without …. I can guarantee you it is a very long list—so what is wrong with just writing for the sake of writing?

The creative wound is a specific type of emotional injury that writers and other artists may experience when their work is harshly criticised, dismissed or devalued. This kind of negative feedback, especially when it comes from someone in a position of authority or influence, can be deeply discouraging and damaging to a writer's self-esteem and motivation.

When confronted with this attitude, we may internalise the criticism and doubt our own abilities and the worth of our creative pursuits. You may feel shame, embarrassment or a sense of failure, leading you to stop writing altogether or to continue writing in secret, hidden away from potential judgement.

The creative wound can have long-lasting effects on your confidence and productivity. It may lead to writer's block, self-censorship, or a reluctance to share your work with others. Some may even abandon their craft entirely, believing that their efforts are futile or that they lack the necessary talent.

Remember that taste is subjective and that even the most celebrated authors have faced rejection and criticism throughout their careers. Many successful writers have learned to view criticism as an inevitable part of the creative process and have developed resilience in the face of rejection. Stephen King, for example, has famously said, 'If you write (or paint or dance or sculpt or sing, I suppose), someone will try to make you feel lousy about it, that's all.'

To overcome the creative wound caused by criticism, you can:

- Seek support from fellow writers, friends or family members who believe in your work. Join a writing group, not a critique group. Find other writers online. Start with Facebook—find me there and join me online for Zoom writing sessions. Links will be in the back of this book. Attend writing retreats, conferences or even start your own writing group in your local library.

- Reframe criticism as an opportunity for growth and learning rather than a personal attack. With the caveat that the criticism comes from a qualified source such as an editor, mentor, writing coach. 'Self-proclaimed book enthusiasts' should never be entertained. Treat any criticism with the attention its source deserves.

- Develop a strong sense of self-validation and trust in your own creative instincts.

- Most importantly—keep writing! No matter what, keep going.

Ultimately, the creative wound caused by harsh criticism is a painful but often unavoidable part of the writing life. By cultivating a strong sense of self-belief, surrounding yourself with supportive allies, and persevering in the face of adversity, you can learn to overcome this challenge and continue to create with passion and purpose.

Writing

Exercise

Write on each topic for ten minutes. Take more time if the words keep coming, but ensure you write on each for at least ten minutes.

1. *Tell me about your creative wound. Where did it come from?*

2. *How can you use the pain?*

3. *In what way does writing heal you?*

I CAN'T BE
A WRITER

'Perfectionism is the voice of the oppressor,
the enemy of the people. It will keep you cramped
and insane your whole life, and it is the main obstacle
between you and a shitty first draft.'

Anne Lamott (1994)

What would my mother, father, husband, wife, friends, kids say if they read that? For the longest time I would destroy my writing, for fear of someone reading it. This didn't come from nowhere. When I was in my early twenties, I wrote a scene, a love scene completely fictional, about a girl seducing a young man from the inland revenue service centre. I wrote it in the first person. She was a dirty seductress, if you understand my meaning, and nothing like me at all. My boyfriend at the time read it and became very upset. Where I thought I wrote a great out-of-body scene, he said it was disgusting … saying he had never read anything so disgusting before …

I was attending a creative writing course at Albany TAFE, my teacher was trying to get into Mills & Boon and encouraged us to do the same. He was a short man, always wore a wool vest, checked shirt and tie. I can't remember his name, but he excitedly told us we could make between $10,000 and $15,000 a book. He said it was formula writing, it was 1992, and he made us believe it was possible. My wage then was $20,000 a year, with overtime. Two books a year would make me more and I would be a writer! He talked about the different genres. Sex sells, he said, and I believed him. I dug deeper. The internet wasn't what it was today, so I took pages of notes on everything he told us. I wanted it. It was a way that I could become a writer. I had been told all my life I would make a good waitress, that I was attractive but not essentially pretty, and if I was lucky I would meet a man who was kind to me and my plain disposition, and I would work until the children arrived and then retire to spend all my good years looking after them. I couldn't be a writer, I was no Agatha Christie, for crying out loud I wasn't even English! The cheek!

As hard as I tried to see the sexual in ordinary situations, to bring out passion where none existed, I wasn't any good, not that I showed anyone who mattered. Because my partner told me so. It was disgusting. It made him feel sick so how could anything come to any good? Mills & Boon would never be interested in my 'dirty stories'. I tried writing articles, light upbeat material for *Woman's Day* and *New Idea*. I sent them off and occasionally got a rejection letter. At least they didn't say it was disgusting. But I buried it a little deeper and set to work at the London Hotel in Albany. Notebook in my bag I took to writing sad poetry about abandonment in my quiet moments. I read books about writing and took a few correspondence courses and basically decided I would stick to poetry. Prose was too hard and obviously I was crap at it.

A poem could be quick, sharp and heartfelt. I could heap a world of emotion in just a few words. I would roll them around, play with the metre, get the sound and meaning just right. I was a happy hobbyist. Very few people were allowed access to my poetry. I kept this book close to my chest, away from the sight of most of the world. It was none of their business.

The internet came, slowly at first, then all at once. Suddenly, there were blogs and online forums, places where people shared their thoughts and stories without fear of rejection letters or disgusted looks.

I remember the first time I stumbled upon a writing community online. It was like finding a hidden oasis in the desert of my isolation. Here were people—thousands of them—who understood the ache to put words on paper, the fear of sharing, the dream of being heard. They wrote about everything: their lives, their fantasies, their pain, their joy. And none of it was disgusting.

At first, I just lurked, reading others' work with a mix of envy and awe. But slowly, tentatively, I began to comment. To encourage. To critique. And in doing so, I found my voice again. Not the voice of the seductress or the romance writer or the women's magazine columnist, but my voice. Raw, uncertain, but undeniably mine.

One day, I posted a poem. Just a short one, called "Why?" I closed the page immediately after, sure that when I returned, I'd find nothing but scorn, or worse, indifference.

When I gathered the courage to look hours later, I found comments. Kind ones. Thoughtful ones. People who saw something in my words, who wanted to know more. It was like a door creaking open, letting in a sliver of light.

I wrote more. The more I wrote, the more I realised that being a writer wasn't about making thousands of dollars or fitting into someone else's formula. It was about having something to say and finding the courage to say it. It was about connecting, about touching someone's heart with your words, even if that heart was yours.

Because that's the thing I've finally learned: being a writer isn't about publication or praise or pay cheques. It's about writing. It's about showing up to the page, day after day, and pouring your heart out in ink. It's about being brave enough to say this is me, this is my truth.

I'm not Agatha Christie. I'm not even a Mills & Boon author. I'm just me, a woman from Adelaide with a notebook full of words and a head full of stories. And you know what? That's enough. That's more than enough. That's everything.

Writing
Exercise

1. *Make a list of everything you have already written. General categories are fine: poetry, articles, essays, novels.*

2. *What have you planned to write? Write a list of everything to come.*

3. *Name the writing projects you are yet to finish.*

4. *Where do you want to start? What is the first or next project you want to have done completely, from idea to draft, to holding the finished book in your hand?*

Why?
Because it robs my day of happiness,
I am crying with the rain.
Pain. Heart torn.
Cracked apart.
This is it.
Hide. Run.

Sobbing, cleansing but
no solution. Run.
Can't face angry shadows again.
I am not strong. Was never strong.

Eyes bloodshot.
It hurts to see. Everything is blurred.
Reasoning and tenderness,
too late, too raw, not heard. Run.

Breasts hurt, halted breath.
Happiness torn.
No match, no dream fulfilled.
Where is happy family?
Endless joy, contentment, nil.

CHANGE YOUR MINDSET

'Recognising that people's reactions don't belong to you is the only sane way to create. If people enjoy what you've created, terrific. If people ignore what you've created, too bad. If people misunderstand what you've created, don't sweat it. And what if people absolutely hate what you've created? What if people attack you with savage vitriol, and insult your intelligence, and malign your motives, and drag your good name through the mud? Just smile sweetly and suggest—as politely as you possibly can—that they go make their own fucking art. Then stubbornly continue making yours.'

Elizabeth Gilbert

I would mentally freeze when people asked me what I did. Most recently, I worked with my husband in our carpentry business. I took care of the admin, in between learning and building my writing practice, writing and publishing my books, becoming a professional editor and writing coach. I have had many jobs besides this to pay the bills: shop assistant, barmaid, bar manager, massage therapist, reiki master, aromatherapist, trade assistant, tool tagger, bookkeeper, pet sitter, merchandiser, receptionist, karate instructor, yoga teacher, copywriter. It took me all my working life to get to where I am now, little steps moving forward. Little habits, every day is what matters and what counts. Change your mindset. You picked up this book because you are a writer. Time to start acting like one.

My career path has been a vibrant tapestry of experiences, each contributing to my unique perspective as a writer and mentor. From my early days in retail and hospitality, to exploring holistic practices, I've worn many hats. This diverse professional background has shaped my approach to writing and teaching. Each job, each experience, has been a stepping stone, contributing to my growth not just as a writer, but as a person.

My path to a full-time writing business is marked by persistence and gradual progress. I firmly believe in the power of small, consistent habits. Every day spent writing, every small step forward, has mattered and counted towards my ultimate goal.

Now, I encourage you to embrace a mindset shift. I challenge you to recognise and accept your identity as a writer, regardless of publication status.

Write this and keep it somewhere you can regularly see it—I Am a Writer!

This powerful affirmation serves as a call to action, urging you to take yourself and your craft seriously, to make time for your passion, and to approach your writing with the dedication and professionalism it deserves.

The path to becoming a writer is rarely linear, but every experience along the way can enrich your writing and fuel your creative fire.

Writing

Exercise

1. *What will you say to people who ask you questions about being a writer?*

    ▢   *What do you write?*

    ▢   *Would I have read your work?*

    ▢   *Have you published anything?*

    ▢   *Where do you get your ideas?*

    ▢   *Is it your full-time job?*

    ▢   *How long have you been writing?*

    ▢   *Who is your favourite author or what's your favourite book?*

    ▢   *Are you working on anything right now?*

    ▢   *Is it hard to get published?*

    ▢   *Do you have an agent or do you self-publish?*

    ▢   *Can I read some of your work?*

In your notebook, write each question across the top of your page and explore your answer. You may like to answer for you now and then again as your future self. Explore the possibilities.

IMPOSTER
SYNDROME

'Ask yourself in the most silent hour of your night:
must I write? Dig into yourself for a deep answer.
And if this answer rings out in assent, if you meet this
solemn question with a strong, simple 'I must,' then build
your life in accordance with this necessity.'

Rainer Maria Rilke

After my son was born in 1995, I set up a home business as a
massage therapist, offering massage, aromatherapy and reiki
treatments. I became a teacher and wrote training manuals
about aromatherapy, reiki and massage. But still, I wasn't
a writer.

I started working with my husband, keeping the books,
we took over a karate club and the internet was here. I wrote
purchase orders, property reports and newsletters for the
karate club, still I wasn't a writer. There is a pattern here: the
internet came, Blogger, then WordPress, and I was a blogger.
I created websites, wrote copy other people read and I wrote
ad copy for the businesses. I took more courses and little by

little I started to look like a writer. Finally, there was some practical sense to my pursuits. No one could say it was a waste of time. But we needed more money. I started a business as a pet sitter. After I took care of the animals' needs, I spent some time writing in my notebook, notes of ideas and plans for projects I wanted to do. When I walked the dogs or drove between jobs, I would listen to podcasts—*A Little Bird Told Me* (Phillipa Willets), *The Creative Penn* (Joanna Penn) and *SPF Show* (Mark Dawson and James Blatch).

Still, when my husband said that being a writer was nothing more than a pipe dream, it hurt. But I had nothing to defend it with. Sure, I had made a few bucks on Google Ads from my blogging, but nothing to brag about, believe me.

It was like a sickness, this writing, this constantly pursuing something. Always writing. At the time I didn't care what I wrote, I just wanted to be a writer. I tried to turn it into something profitable. I learned more about ad copy, more about promotions, blog posts, Facebook and how to hook and manipulate readers into buying what was being sold.

Then I enrolled in my first NANOWRIMO. *National Novel Writing Month* allows me to write without thinking. I am a discovery writer. I will begin with only a faint idea of what I am going to write and away I go. The rush of NANOWRIMO stops my mind from getting in the way. With a goal of writing fifty thousand words in thirty days, there is no time to think about the colour of her hair or the sway of a walk. You just have to write. You have to get your words on to the paper and get it done. Basically, you have to get below the bullshit, the things you think you must write, the things you think you should say. You just have to let your characters speak without judgement and write. Nano is the best tool I have found for getting myself out of the way and putting words on a page. Similarly to what I had to do to get this book written, I have to cleave open and lay myself bare on the page.

I wrote a book called *Allison*, targeted at the romantic/suspense market. Problem was, I didn't know what to do next. How do you edit? Despite everything I had read, I still had no clue what to do.

Forever practical for no other reason than to justify my pursuit, I kept pushing, kept writing, kept learning. But the voice in my head, the one that whispered, *'You're not a real writer,'* never quite went away. It was there when I hit publish on a blog post, when I sent out a newsletter, when I stared at the unedited manuscript of *Allison* gathering digital dust on my hard drive.

I was in a strange limbo. I was writing—constantly, obsessively—but I couldn't call myself a writer. The words were there, flowing from my fingers, filling notebooks and word documents and websites, but they felt insubstantial. Like they didn't count. Because real writers, they got paid, right? They had agents and book deals and their names on glossy covers in bookshop windows.

I remember sitting at my kitchen table late one night, surrounded by sleeping dogs (the perks of being a pet sitter), my laptop open to yet another writing course I'd signed up for. This one promised to teach me how to 'write to market'—how to craft stories that would sell, that would finally make me a real writer. I was tired, so tired, but I couldn't stop. Because what if this was the key? What if this course, this technique, this secret formula was the thing that would finally unlock the door to writerdom?

Even as I took notes, even as I nodded along to the instructor's confident assertions about what readers want, a part of me rebelled. Was this really what I wanted? To contort my words, my stories, my voice into something marketable? To chase trends and algorithms instead of my truth?

I thought back to those early days, to the child who wrote stories, the teen who wrote about her love, the woman who poured her heart into secret poems. They didn't care about markets or sales or even readers. They wrote because they had to, because the words burned inside them, demanding to be set free.

And yet the practical side of me, the side that balanced books and ran businesses and raised children, couldn't let go of the idea that writing should be more than just a hobby. That it should contribute, should matter in some tangible way.

I closed the laptop, rubbed my eyes. Outside, the moon hung low and heavy, casting long shadows across the yard. In that moment, I felt like a shadow myself—neither here nor there, neither writer nor non-writer. An imposter in both worlds.

I looked down at my notebook, at the scribbled ideas and half-formed stories. I Thought of the blogs I had written, the manuals I'd crafted, the newsletters I'd sent out into the world. Each word a tiny act of creation, of connection. Each sentence a step on this winding, confusing, beautiful path. And I realised something. Being a writer isn't a destination. Maybe it's not something you become, like flipping a switch or crossing a finish line. Maybe it's something you do, day after day, word after word, whether or not anyone is watching. Maybe the only real imposters are the ones who stop writing, who let the fear or the doubt or practicality silence their voices.

I picked up my pen. The dogs sighed in their sleep. And I wrote, not because it was practical or profitable, but because I am a writer and I had something to say. Because in that moment, in the quiet of the night with only the moon as my witness, the words were there, and I was there to catch them.

And maybe, just maybe, that was enough.

Writing
Exercise

What kind of writer are you? Tell me how you write, what you write, and the gifts you have received from writing. Go ahead and write now for ten minutes.

TAMING THE MONKEY MIND

'You are where your mind is.'

Radhanath Swami

My mind is a circus, and the monkeys are running the show. While writing this book, I have cleaned my fridge, my oven, sorted the sock basket, re-potted the plants on my porch, painted a streetscape, called my husband, texted my friends, my children, walked around the block seventeen times, did some online shopping, abandoned a few shopping carts and made hundreds of cups of teas. Each time I grasp at a coherent sentence, another chattering simian of distraction steals my attention. The blank page stares back at me, a silent judge of my mental menagerie. I take a deep breath. Sometimes, I manage to corral my thoughts into something resembling a story. Other times, I'm left exhausted, having written nothing but a to-do list and a reminder to google 'how long can bananas last in the fridge?' That is my monkey mind— forever swinging between brilliance and banality, hoping to catch the right vine of inspiration before the next distraction comes along.

As writers, we have all experienced those moments when our minds seem to have a life of their own, jumping from thought to thought like a playful monkey swinging through trees. This phenomenon, aptly named 'monkey mind', can be a significant obstacle in our creative process.

The term monkey mind originates from Buddhist principles and describes a state where our thoughts are unsettled, restless and capricious. For me, this manifests as an inability to focus, with my attention constantly shifting between ideas, worries, distractions, family obligations, TikTok and other random scrolling.

How Monkey Mind Affects Writing

- **Disrupted Flow:** just as you're getting into the rhythm of your writing, your mind throws a random thought your way, breaking your concentration.

- **Perfectionism Paralysis:** the monkey mind often fuels self-doubt, making you overthink every word and sentence.

- **Procrastination:** with your thoughts scattered, it becomes easier to put off writing in favour of less demanding tasks.

- **Reduced Creativity:** constant mental chatter can drown out the subtle voice of inspiration and intuition.

- **Exhaustion:** battling with a restless mind is mentally draining, leaving less energy for actual writing.

Tame the Monkey Mind

- **Mindfulness Meditation:** practise short mindfulness sessions before writing. This helps calm the mind and improves focus. Even five to ten minutes can make a significant difference.

- **Create a Ritual:** establish a pre-writing routine that signals to your brain it's time to focus. This could be brewing a cup of tea, lighting a candle, loading the dishwasher or doing some light stretches.

- **Use the Pomodoro Technique:** work in focused twenty-five-minute intervals followed by short breaks. This gives the monkey mind some playtime without letting it dominate your writing session.

- **Brain Dump:** before you start writing, spend a few minutes jotting down all the random thoughts occupying your mind. This clears mental space for your writing.

- **Set Clear Goals:** have a clear objective for each writing session. When the mind wanders, gently guide it back to the task at hand.

- **Create a Distraction-Free Environment:** turn off notifications, use website blockers, and create a physical space conducive to focused work.

- **Practise Acceptance:** sometimes, fighting the monkey mind only strengthens it. Learn to acknowledge distracting thoughts without engaging them, letting them pass like clouds in the sky.

- **Regular Exercise:** physical activity can help settle a restless mind. Consider a brief workout or walk before writing sessions.

- **Adequate Sleep:** a well-rested mind is less prone to wandering. Prioritise good sleep hygiene to support your writing practice.

- **Freewriting:** when the monkey mind is particularly active, try freewriting. Let your thoughts flow on to the page without judgement, which can lead to unexpected creative insights.

While the monkey mind can be disruptive, it's also a source of creativity. The key is learning to direct its energy productively. Sometimes the most original ideas come from seemingly random connections made by wandering minds.

The goal isn't to eliminate the monkey mind entirely, but to establish a harmonious relationship with it. By acknowledging its presence and implementing strategies to manage it, you can harness its creative potential while maintaining the focus needed to bring your writing projects to fruition.

Remember, every writer grapples with mental distractions. Successful writers aren't those who never experience monkey mind, but those who have learned to work with it effectively. With practice and patience, you can turn your monkey mind into a powerful ally.

Monkey Mind at Work

Writing
Exercise

Name your monkey and write a letter to them. Talk about how you would like to manage the relationship from now on. What limits and freedoms are you willing to give your monkey?

SILENCING THE INNER EDITOR

'You don't start out writing good stuff. You start out writing crap and thinking it's good stuff, and then gradually you get better at it. That's why I say one of the most valuable traits is persistence.'

Octavia Butler

I had a stack of beautiful, unused notebooks. I was afraid to spoil them with my crappy words. I didn't know what I was doing. I wasn't capable of writing anything worthy of defacing these beauties. This precious lined paper, pressed between covered cardboard, emboldened with rich designs or worse, words of wisdom—*Don't give up on your dreams. The best way to predict the future is to create it. Fill your paper with the breathings of your heart …*

So where could I write? You guessed it, nowhere. Until I counted fifteen unused notebooks on my shelf. Away I went, with a pen in hand, and filled them all. It turns out it wasn't a waste of pressed paper and cardboard. It was the beginning of getting my writing down, all of it. The good, the bad and the ugly. The misspelled words and the scribble-like doctor's handwriting I fall into when my brain moves too fast for my hand.

I am a long way removed from the poetry book I treasured in my early twenties. I wouldn't write directly into it. I would work the poem out on scrap paper first and transcribe it in my best handwriting. As if it was something holy and beyond receiving my everyday meanderings. I didn't have a computer then, but when I finally got one, those poems ended up cloistered on a hard drive, rarely seeing the light of day.

Thirty years on and I have a type—A5 ruled Moleskine notebook and Lamy fountain pen with a converting cartridge I can refill straight from the bottle for writing practice at home and a good old Bic four-colour fat pen when I am out and about. I am not a dinosaur. I will use my computer when working on a specific piece. But writing practice needs us to engage fully, and the best way to do that is by handwriting words on a page. Notebooks and pens are more convenient, slip easily into your bag, are inexpensive and wonderfully tactile.

Stream-of-consciousness writing stands out as a powerful tool for unleashing creativity and accessing the deepest recesses of the mind. Fully embracing this technique can be challenging because of the persistent voice of the inner editor.

Stream-of-consciousness is a narrative device that attempts to portray the multitudinous thoughts and feelings passing through your mind. As a writing exercise, it involves writing continuously, without regard for grammar, structure, or even coherence, allowing thoughts to flow freely on to the page.

The inner editor, that critical voice in your head that scrutinises every word you write, plays a crucial role in refining and polishing your work. During the initial stages of creative writing, particularly in stream-of-consciousness exercises, this voice can be more hindrance than help.

Why the Inner Editor Interferes

- **Perfectionism:** the desire for flawless prose from the get-go

- **Fear of judgement:** worry about how others might perceive your raw thoughts

- **Habit:** years of focusing on grammar and structure in writing

- **Lack of trust:** doubting the value of unfiltered thoughts

Techniques for Silencing the Inner Editor

- **Set a timer:** give yourself a specific time frame (ten minutes) for writing. The time pressure can help override the editor's voice.

- **Use freewriting:** start with a prompt and write continuously without stopping to revise or correct.

- **Practise mindfulness:** before writing, spend a few moments in mindful meditation to centre yourself and clear your mind.

- **Create a 'No Judgement' zone:** establish a mental space where all thoughts are welcome, no matter how strange or unconventional.

- **Write by hand:** the physical act of writing can create a stronger connection between thought and expression, bypassing the inner critic.

- **Use stream-of-consciousness prompts:** start with prompts that encourage free association and random thoughts.

- **Embrace imperfection:** remind yourself that the goal is exploration, not perfection.

- **Write in a different environment:** a change of scenery can help break habitual thought patterns.

- **Use the 'Shitty First Draft' technique:** acknowledge that your first draft is meant to be rough and unpolished.

- **Practise regularly:** like any skill, silencing the inner editor gets easier with consistent practice.

The Benefits of Ignoring the Inner Editor

- **Increased creativity:** access to a wider range of ideas and associations

- **Emotional release:** a cathartic outlet for unexpressed thoughts and feelings

- **Improved writing flow:** development of a more natural, authentic voice

- **Self-discovery:** insights into your subconscious mind and hidden thoughts

- **Overcoming writer's block:** a technique to push past creative obstacles

From Stream to Polished Prose

While stream-of-consciousness writing is valuable in itself, it can also serve as a foundation for more structured work. Once you've completed your free-flowing session:

- **Review:** read through your writing without judgement

- **Highlight:** mark interesting ideas or phrases that stand out

- **Develop:** use these highlights as seeds for more structured pieces

- **Edit:** now, and only now, let your inner editor have its say

Stream-of-consciousness writing is about embracing the chaotic, non-linear nature of human thought. By learning to temporarily silence your inner editor, you open yourself to a world of creative possibilities. Remember, the goal is not to produce perfect prose, but to explore the depths of your mind and imagination.

In the words of Natalie Goldberg, author of *Writing Down the Bones*, 'First thoughts have tremendous energy. It is the way the mind first flashes on something. The internal censor usually squelches them, so we live in the realm of second and third thoughts, thoughts on thought, twice and three times removed from the direct connection of the first fresh flash.'

The next time you sit down to write, give yourself permission to ignore that critical voice. Let your thoughts flow freely and see where the stream takes you. You might be surprised by the treasures you discover when you allow yourself to write without constraints.

Writing
Exercise

Spend ten minutes writing on each question.

1. *What are you thinking about right now?*

2. *What is it that you don't want to think about?*

3. *Tell me what you will fill your notebooks with.*

BALANCING CREATIVITY AND CRAFT

'The greatest gift of the garden is the restoration of
the five senses. The garden is a sensual place, and its
sensuality draws us in, enticing us with fragrant flowers,
tempting us with luscious tomatoes, charming us with the
melody of a bird's song. But more than that, through its
ever-changing beauty and abundant hope, the garden
engages us intellectually and enlightens us spiritually.'

Fran Sorin

When I first started writing, my process was like tending to
an overgrown, chaotic garden. Ideas sprouted everywhere,
tangled and wild. I'd spend hours nurturing these wild
growths, only to find myself lost in a maze of weeds. I had to
learn to balance this creative abundance with the structured
care of craft.

Writers often find themselves tending to different aspects
of their craft, much like gardeners nurturing various parts of
their garden. To better understand these aspects, think of them

as two distinct garden spaces, each symbolising a different component of the writing process. This idea, presents a framework for understanding the dual nature of creative writing.

Imagine your writing process as a garden with two distinct areas. One area is a wild, untamed meadow representing unbridled creativity, while the other is a well-manicured formal garden embodying disciplined craft. Understanding and balancing these two spaces is crucial for any writer seeking to produce compelling work.

The Wild Meadow: Creativity

The first area is a wild, unpredictable and vibrant meadow. This space represents:

- **Raw Creativity:** the sprouting of new ideas and imaginative leaps

- **Emotional Truth:** the ability to cultivate deep feelings and experiences

- **Intuition:** following natural growth patterns and unexpected connections

- **Passion:** the fertile soil that nourishes our writing

- **Originality:** allowing unique and exotic plants to thrive

The Formal Garden: Craft

The second area is a well-planned, structured and carefully maintained formal garden. This space embodies:

- **Technical Skill:** mastery of pruning techniques (grammar, syntax and structure)

- **Narrative Technique:** understanding the landscape design (plot, character development, and pacing)

- **Editing and Revision:** the ability to refine and shape raw growth

- **Genre Conventions:** knowledge of popular garden styles and visitor expectations

- **Consistency:** maintaining a cohesive garden design throughout

The art of writing lies in tending both garden spaces effectively. Here's how they interact:

The Creative Planting

During the initial writing phase, you often start in the wild meadow. This is where you:

- Allow seeds of imagination to scatter freely

- Let ideas grow without immediate pruning

- Explore unexpected flora in your narrative landscape

The Craft of Cultivation

Once the initial growth is complete, you step into the formal garden. This is when you:

- Apply your horticultural skills to shape the raw material

- Ensure a coherent garden layout and logical pathways

- Polish your garden features for maximum visual impact

The Seasonal Cycle

Throughout the writing process, you'll find yourself alternating between these two spaces:

- Letting creativity bloom, then applying craft to shape it

- Using landscaping techniques to overcome barren patches, then allowing new growth to flourish

Challenges in Balancing the Two Gardens

- **Overemphasis on the wild meadow:** resulting in an overgrown, chaotic landscape

- **Overemphasis on the formal garden:** leading to a sterile, overly manicured space

- **Timing issues:** pruning too early, stunting creative growth

- **Perfectionism:** over-cultivating the formal garden, stifling natural beauty

Harmonising the Two Gardens

- **Separate planting and pruning:** have distinct times for free growth and for shaping

- **Nurture wildflowers:** regular exercises to enrich the creative soil

- **Study horticulture:** continuous learning to refine your gardening skills

- **Visit diverse gardens:** expose yourself to various styles to inspire both spaces

- **Find your climate:** discover the balance that works best for your writing ecosystem

- **Embrace natural growth:** allow the wild meadow to flourish in early stages

- **Set clear landscaping goals:** use craft-oriented plans to guide your creative exploration

The Evolving Ecosystem

As you grow as a writer, you'll find that the relationship between your two garden spaces changes:

- The wild meadow may develop its own natural patterns over time

- The formal garden might incorporate more organic, free-flowing elements

- You'll develop a more intuitive sense of when to let each space flourish

By recognising and nurturing both your creative and craft-oriented areas, you can produce writing that is both lush with inspiration and elegantly structured. Remember, great writing isn't about choosing between untamed growth and manicured perfection—it's about finding the perfect balance between these two essential spaces.

As you continue your writing journey, pay attention to how these two gardens thrive in your own process. Learn to tend to both, respect their unique characteristics, and cultivate them towards your ultimate goal: creating a compelling, meaningful landscape that resonates with readers.

Writing

Exercise

What is in your wild garden? Write about the seeds you will plant there.

DAILY WRITING PRACTICE

'I write only when inspiration strikes.
Fortunately, it strikes every morning at nine o'clock sharp.'

W. Somerset Maugham

I carry a notebook and pen with me everywhere. In the beginning, I imagined I'd whip them out the second inspiration struck or I heard an enchanting turn of phrase. It's not a romantic relationship, but it's a necessary part of my everyday make-up. They are my constant companion, the tools of my trade.

Despite my commitment to carry these tools, I don't write every day—and that's okay. My goal is to write as often as possible, finding those pockets of time in daily life:

- A stolen half hour in a cafe

- Morning coffee in bed with my notebook

- A quiet moment in the park

- Between laps of my neighbourhood
- While watching television
- During lunch
- Waiting for time to pass

These moments add up. Every month I fill a notebook. It's not necessarily a daily practice, but it's frequent, and that's what matters.

When I sit down to write, I have strategies to get the words flowing:

- Write about the present moment: What's happening with my family? What do I see around me?
- Use timed writing exercises to push past today.
- Explore project ideas that have been percolating in my mind.
- Turn to my list of writing prompts in the back of my notebook.

Here are a few prompts from the back of my notebook:

- I remember when I was a child
- The way my mother smelt
- The day I fell in love
- What it will feel like to be old
- The thing I regret the most

- I wish I had …
- The rain
- The sun
- The mind
- The moon

Let the writing take you wherever it needs to go. Mix fiction and non-fiction, explore the human condition. This practice isn't about producing a novel, a play or a collection of poetry. It's about polishing your tools: your mind, your eyes and your ears.

To write well, you need more than just words and grammar. You need to understand yourself and who you're writing for.

From my notebook:

'I want to write stories about women and the female condition. To do this successfully, I need to understand myself, how my experiences shape me and direct my actions. Some of it is deep and meaningful and tears open the heart of me. Other parts are as simple as how I react when I stub my toe.'

Every experience, every emotion you acknowledge, becomes part of your writing psyche. It might not emerge immediately, but it's there, waiting to breathe life into a character or a scene. Trust in the power of emergence—no knowledge or understanding is ever useless to a writer.

Frequent writing practice is about consistency, not perfection. It's about showing up for yourself and your craft as often as you can, whether that's daily or not. Don't wait for all your ducks to be in a row—they never will be. Instead, embrace the imperfect moments, capture the world around you, and keep filling those notebooks. Remember, everything you need is already within you. Your job is to keep tapping into that well, as often as you can, and let your unique voice flow on to the page.

Writing
Exercise

What is directly in front of you at this minute? Capture every detail, including the temperature, the noise you can hear, what can you smell, how does the air taste?

ESTABLISH A WRITING ROUTINE

'I have forced myself to begin writing when I've been utterly exhausted, when I've felt my soul as thin as a playing card, when nothing has seemed worth enduring for another five minutes ... and somehow the activity of writing changes everything. Or appears to do so.'

Joyce Carol Oates

Writing every day is not always a viable option. We may intend to set the alarm clock for five o'clock each morning and get up and write two thousand words before the house stirs. We start out okay, then we have a late night. One of the kids was sick, we caught an extra episode of that Netflix series and so on. We don't get out of bed when the alarm goes off, then we miss another day and so on and so on. Anything can stand it our way. It is just writing, right? No one is waiting with bated breath for us to finish. Chances are no one will care if you write. No one. They may offer courteous platitudes of, 'Oh, that's a shame, never mind. You will find another hobby.' (Insert scream here!)

Look at your schedule now. If you don't have a schedule, draw one up now. It is well overdue. Include work, family, leisure, exercise and study commitments. See the seven-day schedule at the back of this book.

Look at anything you can take out—besides exercise, sleep and self-care. Can you watch an hour less of television every day? If you catch a bus or train to work, can you use that time to write? Could you head to work a little earlier and stop off at a library or coffee shop and write there before heading to your day job? Be creative if you need to and find reasonable pockets of writing time. If you can find seven sessions, leave out two for manoeuvring room. You can still write for seven days, but you won't always be able to. If you find five, block out four. If you can only find one … book it in and use the last five minutes of that one attempting to find another one. And keep building until you have three to five writing sessions booked in every week.

Book it in like you would any other appointment with your doctor, dentist, hairdresser. Block this time out of your everyday availability. You wouldn't expect to call your partner while they are at the gym or playing netball? So don't feel bad for scheduling this time to do the one thing your mind, body and soul are craving to do. Guard this time with all your might, defend your right to write!

You wouldn't want to miss a coffee date with a friend. Your writing is that friend. Take yourself out for coffee, tea or a juice on a set day every week and keep that appointment as much as possible and if you miss a session, make it up. You owe it to yourself and to your writing. Make the time, even when it seems impossible. Cross out all the excuses: I have work, I have to clean up, I have to cook, I have a family to take care of, I have to take care of my mother, my father, my pets, my church, my this and my that. You have responsibilities yes, but I am going to argue that you also have a responsibility to your writing. If you don't listen to the urge, it won't go away, it will fester and turn into a regret. Is it really too much to ask for a once-a-week appointment with your notebook and pen?

If you are really struggling to find the time, let the habit take, then grow. Just like laundry, grocery shopping, squeeze it into your day. Toni Morrison said, 'Write around the edges of your day,' and you can, for now. Carry your notebook and pen with you, get some words down waiting for the kids to come out of school, while watching television, waiting to see the doctor, find impromptu writing sessions.

It starts by getting comfortable with the practice. Write about anything. If you are unsure where to start, write about what is directly in front of you.

Writing
Exercise

1. *Describe your ideal writing day.*

2. *Make the necessary plans for this to happen.*

A WRITING SPACE

'The art of writing is the art of applying the seat of the
pants to the seat of the chair.'

Mary Heaton Vorse

Do you remember Colin Firth's character in *Love Actually*,
writing by a lake in France on his old manual typewriter,
while the housekeeper brings him tea and too many cakes?
This isn't the way for most of us. I have written in my car, in
waiting rooms, outside dance classes, karate classes, at school
pickups, in cafes and in my little kitchen office. Be fluid in the
expectation of where and when you will write. Be prepared to
write on any medium—notebook, phone, laptop, computer,
iPad, random piece of paper, shop receipt, napkins and half-
filled exercise books. Don't be precious, get the words down.

Stephen King wrote *Carrie* while working in a laundry;
JK Rowling wrote the *Harry Potter* books in cafes around
Edinburgh; Roald Dahl wrote in his garden shed; Elizabeth

Gilbert writes at a plain desk surrounded by a few items she loves and a box of index cards she has prepared her novel on; Joanna Penn writes in cafes around her town of Bath; Natalie Goldberg writes at home; in cafes, libraries, under trees, basically everywhere.

This is my home office. It is at the end of my kitchen. It sits on a rug that measures 160 cm x 230 cm. You can see the kitchen bench in the left-hand corner of the photo. I have honestly just stood up and taken this picture with my iPhone.

This is the space I have etched out of my family home. It is perfect. Close to the kettle for tea, near snacks, and household distractions.

Sometimes it is better and more productive to get away from the house to write, but I can't always do that, and honestly I am just happy to have this little Ikea-built cubicle to work in. Everything I need is here.

Write at Home

- Home office: a dedicated room or corner equipped with a desk, comfortable chair, good lighting, and storage space for books and writing materials. This set-up provides a quiet, distraction-free environment conducive to focused writing.

- Kitchen table: the kitchen table can serve as a simple yet effective writing space, particularly if you enjoy being close to the heart of the home. You can clear off a portion of the table and set up your laptop or writing materials when it's time to write.

- Cosy armchair: a comfortable armchair in a quiet corner of the living room or bedroom can be a great spot if you prefer a more relaxed, intimate writing environment. You can use a lap desk or a nearby side table to hold your writing materials.

- Backyard or balcony: when the weather permits, writing outdoors can be refreshing and inspiring. Setting up a small table and chair in the backyard or on a balcony can provide a pleasant change of scenery and help stimulate creativity.

- Converted closet: if you have limited space, converting a closet into a tiny writing nook can be a clever solution. By installing a small desk, shelves and adequate lighting, a closet can be transformed into a cosy, private writing area.

Outside of the Home

- Coffee shops: many writers find the ambient noise and energy of a coffee shop stimulating for their creativity. Some coffee shops even cater to writers by offering comfortable seating, power outlets, and Wi-Fi.

- Libraries: libraries provide a quiet, studious atmosphere that can be perfect if you need to concentrate. Many libraries also have private study rooms or carrels that writers can use for added privacy.

- Co-working spaces: co-working spaces are shared office environments that can be rented on a daily, weekly, or monthly basis. They provide you with a professional workspace, opportunities for networking, and a sense of community.

- Parks and outdoor spaces: writing in nature can be inspiring and refreshing. Parks, gardens and other outdoor spaces can provide a peaceful setting for writers to work, especially on nice days.

- Trains, planes and other modes of transportation: writing on trains, planes or even buses can be an efficient use of travel time and can help writers stay focused and avoid distractions.

When you are taking your writing on the road, it is important to be organised and make sure that you have everything you need on hand:

- Laptop or tablet: a portable device for writing and storing your work.

- Notebook and pens/pencils: for jotting down ideas, sketching or writing when you prefer to work offline.

- Chargers and extra batteries: to keep your devices powered up and ready to use.

- USB drive or external hard drive: for backing up your work and transferring files between devices.

- Headphones: to help you focus by blocking out noise or listening to music that inspires you.

- Reference books or writing guides: bring along any books that you find helpful for your writing process, such as a thesaurus, dictionary or style guide. Try to get these online, or on your Kindle so they are easier to carry around.

- Inspirational materials: include items that motivate or inspire you, such as photos, postcards or quotes.

- Snacks and water: pack some healthy snacks and a water bottle to keep your energy levels up while writing.

- Comfortable extras: depending on your preferences, you might want to include items like a small pillow for back support, a lap desk, or a cosy scarf.

- Post-it notes and page markers: these can be handy for marking important pages in your reference books or jotting down quick notes.

- A small pouch or organiser: use this to keep your bag tidy and your smaller items, like pens and USB drives, easily accessible.

Remember, the contents of your writer's go-bag should be tailored to your individual needs and preferences. Consider the type of writing you do, the locations you frequent, and the items that help you feel most comfortable and inspired.

Writing
Exercise

1. *Describe your ideal writing space.*

2. *Where can you write? Make a list of places inside and outside the home.*

3. *Create your own go-bag.*

THE ARTIST DATE: NURTURING YOUR CREATIVE SELF

'For many of us, our inner artists have been waiting to speak with us for years.'

Julia Cameron

I take myself on artist dates to museums and art galleries in the city. I take a train ride into Perth, which offers its own form of entertainment:

- I observe fellow passengers, seeking inspiration in the everyday scenes around me.

- As we travel, I watch the suburbs pass by.

- After crossing the Swan River, I see Kings Park on my left and Perth's skyscrapers on my right.

Upon arriving, I exit the train and walk through the tunnels to Perth Cultural Centre. My destination varies depending on the day:

- Sometimes I'll attend a writing class at the library.

- If there's a new exhibition, I might explore the museum.

- Often, I find myself wandering the art gallery.

- While I'm not an art expert, I know what I like. I enjoy sitting with pieces that capture my interest, but I find equal fascination in observing other visitors and listening to their conversations.

After my cultural exploration, I treat myself to lunch at a nearby cafe. This is where I reflect on my experiences:

- I take out my notebook and write about the morning's adventures.

- It's a chance to process what I've seen and felt.

Post-lunch, my journey continues:

- I walk over the bridge and through Murray Street Mall.

- Down the steps, I find myself at Boffins Books.

- I wander the shelves, happy to lose myself among the titles.

- I select two or three books to take home and add to my to-be-read pile.

- I catch the train home, leaving before the peak hour rush.

Like anything we need to do, we need to refill. We cook for our family. We need to refill the fridge and the pantry, we expend all our energy at work and we sleep at night to recharge, we go to the gym, we refuel our bodies, we eat healthy to stay healthy. Fill your creative bucket. Read, input as much as you can, go see a movie, go to a play, something different, outside of your scope. Linger up and down the aisles of a bookshop, a library, stroll a museum, go visit a country town, eat somewhere new, go to the zoo, volunteer at a dog shelter, sit in a park, watch the sunset, jump into the ocean at sunrise, join the penguins, something that takes you away from your everyday, puts you in a new environment and expands your point of view.

The 'Artist Date' is a concept introduced by Julia Cameron in her book *The Artist's Way.* It is a dedicated block of time, usually two hours or more, that you set aside each week to nurture your inner artist, explore new ideas, and seek inspiration. The purpose of the Artist Date is to refill the creative well, spark the imagination, and encourage playfulness and curiosity.

The key idea behind the Artist Date is that by regularly engaging in fun, spontaneous and enriching activities, you can stimulate your creativity and maintain a sense of enthusiasm and vitality in your artistic practice. It is a form of self-care and self-discovery that allows you to step outside your routine, try new things, and connect with your inner child.

Create Your Artist Date

- Schedule it in advance: treat the Artist Date as a sacred commitment to yourself and your artistic growth. Put it on your calendar and protect that time from other obligations or distractions.

- Choose an activity that interests you: the Artist Date should be something that excites, intrigues or challenges you. It can be anything from visiting a museum, attending a concert, trying a new hobby, or exploring a neighbourhood you've never been to before.

- Do it alone: the Artist Date is meant to be a solo adventure, free from the influence or expectations of others. This solitude allows you to focus on your own thoughts, feelings and experiences without distraction.

- Approach it with an open mind: let go of any preconceived notions or judgements about the activity or yourself. Embrace a sense of curiosity, playfulness and spontaneity, and allow yourself to be surprised by what you discover.

To make time for the Artist Date, you may need to:

- Prioritise it: recognise that nurturing your creativity is just as important as any other commitment or responsibility in your life. Make it a non-negotiable part of your schedule.

- Communicate with others: let your family, friends or colleagues know that you have an appointment with yourself and ask for their support and understanding in honouring that time.

- Be flexible: if your usual Artist Date time doesn't work one week, find another slot that does. The key is to maintain the habit and not let too much time pass between dates.

- Start small: if a whole day feels daunting, begin with a shorter time commitment and gradually work your way up. The important thing is to establish the practice and make it a consistent part of your creative life.

By making the Artist Date a regular practice, you can cultivate a sense of wonder, curiosity and inspiration that can fuel your creative work and keep you engaged and energised over the long term.

Writing
Exercise

Plan your artist date:

1. *Where will you go?*

2. *What will you do?*

READING

'If you want to be a writer, you must do two things above all others: read a lot and write a lot. There's no way around these two things that I'm aware of, no shortcut.'

William Faulkner

I grew up in a household where the only books were Agatha Christie and *Master Detective* magazines. These were the books of choice of my adopted mum, Jean. Everything else was trash or 'not worth the paper it was written on'. Like many kids back in the 1970s, it was the school's library that opened my mind to the world of books.

Reading is not just a pastime for writers; it's an essential part of your craft. The relationship between reading and writing is symbiotic, each nurturing and enhancing the other. Regular reading exposes you to a vast array of words, phrases and linguistic constructions. This exposure naturally enhances a writer's vocabulary and ability to express complex ideas. The more diverse the reading material, the more varied and nuanced your language becomes.

Each author has a unique voice and style. By reading widely, you can observe and analyse different approaches to storytelling, character development, dialogue, and narrative structure. This understanding allows you to experiment with various styles and find your own unique voice. Books are windows to different worlds, cultures and perspectives. This wealth of information serves as a wellspring of inspiration for new ideas, settings and characters.

As we writers read, we naturally analyse the text—considering plot structure, character motivations and thematic elements. This critical thinking enhances our ability to construct and refine our own narratives. Understanding conventional writing rules and techniques through reading allows you to make informed decisions about when and how to break these rules effectively in your own work.

Fiction, in particular, allows writers to step into the shoes of diverse characters. This fosters empathy and emotional intelligence, crucial skills for creating authentic, multidimensional characters and relatable stories.

Reading is not just beneficial for writers—it's indispensable. It's a fundamental tool for growth, learning and inspiration. As Stephen King famously said, 'If you don't have time to read, you don't have the time (or the tools) to write. Simple as that.' For those aspiring to master the art of writing, cultivating a rich and diverse reading habit is not just recommended it's essential.

Writing
Exercise

Read widely, in and outside of your genre. Read craft books and anything else that interests you.

Make a list of books you want to read.

NURTURING
YOUR MIND

'Almost everything will work again
if you unplug it for a few minutes, including you.'

Anne Lamott

In the isolated realm of writing, where ideas transfer from thoughts to paper, it's simple to overlook the person who enables it all—you. As writers, our craft demands much from us mentally and physically. Let's dive into self-care practices that will keep your creativity and well-being in top shape.

Emotional Health: Nurturing the Creative Mind

Embrace Mindfulness.

The writer's mind often races with ideas, plotlines and character voices. While this mental activity fuels our work, it can also lead to stress and anxiety. Incorporate mindfulness practices into your routine:

- Try meditation or deep-breathing exercises to centre your thoughts.

- Practise present-moment awareness during daily activities.

- Use mindfulness apps or guided sessions to get started.

Cultivate a Supportive Community

Writing can be isolating. Combat loneliness by:

- Joining local or online writing groups.

- Attending literary events and workshops.

- Forming a small critique circle with trusted peers.

Set Realistic Goals

Unrealistic expectations can lead to frustration and burnout. Instead:

- Break large projects into manageable tasks.

- Celebrate small victories along the way.

- Use tools like bullet journaling to track progress visually.

Practise Self-Compassion

Writers often face rejection and self-doubt. Counter negative self-talk by:

- Acknowledging that rejection is part of the process, not a reflection of your worth.

- Keeping a 'wins' folder to revisit during tough times.

- Treating yourself with the kindness you'd offer a friend facing similar challenges.

Are you lonely? What do you most need to do for yourself? Write a letter to your writer self and tell them what you are going to do to look after them. Be specific, make appointments with yourself and for yourself and see it through.

CARING FOR THE WRITER'S BODY

'Take care of your body.
It's the only place you have to live.'

Jim Rohn

In 2017, a car carrier truck hit my vehicle as I crossed the Anketell overpass. I'd taken this route countless times before. The truck ran the red light and continued speeding up the Kwinana Freeway. My Ford Mondeo spun out of control, crashing into the pedestrian barrier before lifting off the ground and slamming onto the road and resting in the path of oncoming traffic.

I was lucky. My car was a write-off, but I survived. The crash left me with ongoing neck and hip issues, so I must take care of myself, no matter what I'm doing. Still, I am guilty of neglecting my physical care when working on a project. I am a work in progress, even after all these years. Please look after yourself.

Ergonomics Matter

Long hours at the desk can take a toll. Invest in your workspace:

- Use an ergonomic chair and keyboard to prevent strain.
- Position your screen at eye level to avoid neck pain.
- Consider a standing desk or treadmill desk for variety.

Move Your Body

Regular physical activity boosts creativity and overall health:

- Take short walks between writing sessions.
- Try yoga or stretching to alleviate muscle tension.
- Aim for at least thirty minutes of moderate exercise daily.

Mind Your Posture

Be aware of your body position while writing:

- Set reminders to check and correct your posture.
- Try the 20-20-20 rule: every twenty minutes, look at something twenty feet away for twenty seconds.
- Incorporate back-strengthening exercises into your routine.

Nourish Your Body

Fuelling your body properly enhances mental clarity and energy:

- Stay hydrated; keep a water bottle at your desk.

- Opt for brain-boosting foods like nuts, berries and fatty fish.

- Limit caffeine intake, especially later in the day.

Prioritise Sleep

Quality sleep is crucial for creativity and cognitive function:

- Establish a consistent sleep schedule.

- Create a relaxing bedtime routine.

- Limit screen time before bed to improve sleep quality.

Integrating Self-Care into Your Writing Life

Self-care isn't selfish—it's essential. By taking care of your emotional and physical health, you're investing in your craft. Here are some final tips for integrating self-care into your writing life:

- Schedule self-care activities as you would writing sessions.

- Listen to your body and mind—take breaks when needed.

- Regularly reassess and adjust your self-care routine.

- Remember that taking time for self-care ultimately makes you a better writer.

As writers, our minds and bodies are our most valuable tools. By nurturing both through intentional self-care practices, we not only enhance our well-being but also fuel our creativity and productivity. So, take a deep breath, stretch, and remember: caring for yourself is an integral part of your writing journey.

SIMPLE DESK YOGA

Repeat the entire sequence 3 times at regular intervals throughout your writing day.

With feet flat on the floor, move shoulders away from your ears. Breath in and out of your nose, for 5 breaths.

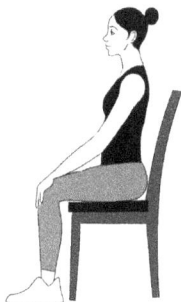

Lift your chin to the sky as you inhale, allowing your back to arch, and chest to come forward.

Exhale, lower your chin to your chest, and round your shoulders. Repeat this seated version of cat-cow 5 times.

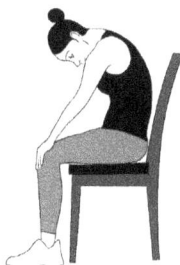

Chair Twists

Hold for 5 Breaths.

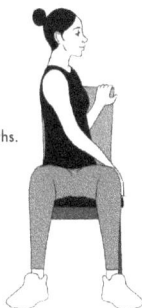

Hold on to the back of your chair or interlace your fingers behind your back. Arch your back, look up and hold for 5 breaths.

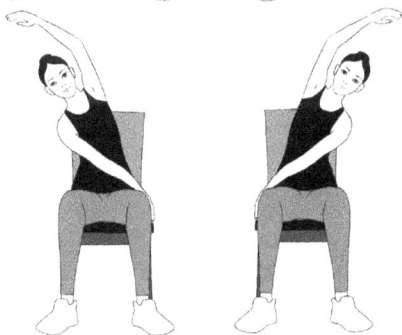

Seated side bends

Hold each side for 5 breaths.

Push hands together,
keep shoulders down.
Hold for 5 breaths.

Hands flat on desk, release head,
move shoulders away from ears.
Hold for 5 breaths.

Interlace fingers behind
your head and gently
push down. Hold for
5 breaths.

Interlace fingers behind
your head. Lift chin to
the sky, arch your back
and hold for 5 breaths.

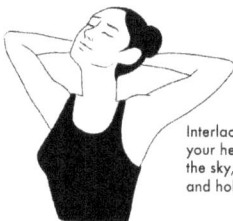

Use the weight of your arm to gently guide
your ear towards your shoulder and hold
for 5 breaths. Repeat on the other side.

Return to a neutral pose
and take a moment to breathe.

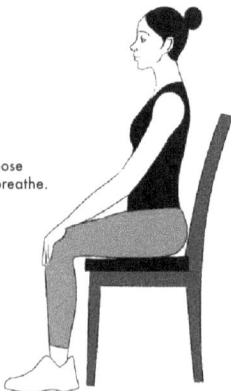

Focus on the movement of breath
in and out of your body.

Writing
Exercise

1. *What do you do now to keep healthy?*

2. *What will you need to change to keep healthy?*

3. *Write a list of things you can add to your life to stay healthy.*

SUSTAINING YOUR CREATIVE WRITING PRACTICE

'A professional writer is an amateur who didn't quite.'

Richard Bach

Writing feels very personal. Even when our goal is to write a novel and be a published author, it is still a very individual pursuit. It feels selfish. It takes us away from our family, our daily routine, our everyday responsibilities. It differs from going to the gym, taking a walk, learning something for work, painting the house, gardening, sewing, and so on.

Few people understand the drive we have to write. The urge to express ourselves with words on a page—to tell a story, to tell stories we design, to create worlds and quests, loves and battles, heartaches and reliefs. Think of how many people in your world take the trouble to read a book, never mind write one.

It may be okay if we took time out for a hairdo, to get our nails done or have a massage—people can relate to that, but tell them you want to sit alone with your computer or your notebook and write for hours and what will they say?

It is easy for them to think that you are boring, a nerd or unsocial. How can you maintain your boundaries without upsetting people you care about just because you want some time alone to write?

When my children were babies, I would try to use their nap time to get a load of housework done then sit and write. *Ah bliss*, I would think, but I can guarantee you the minute my pen hit the paper I would draw a blank and start writing about my day, my hopes and disappointments, it would be a whinge fest despite my best intentions of writing about a story, a character or something I considered being of substance.

I took writing courses, to learn and then to legitimise my creative writing drive. I learned a lot, but I still didn't learn to unleash! To stop being afraid to say I am a writer.

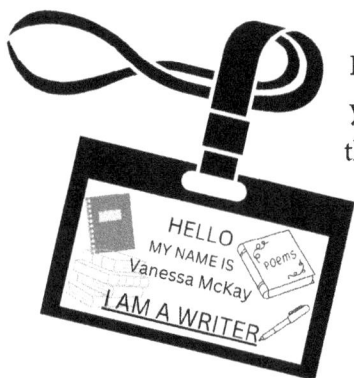

It is easy to get sidetracked, to let yourself and your practice fall by the wayside. Here are some final tips to help you sustain your writing practice:

- Set yourself a goal to write five times a week, or once a week, whatever works for you. Be flexible to reduce the risk of having to throw the entire schedule out.

- Create a dedicated writing space that is comfortable, free of distractions and inspires you to write. It doesn't have to be expensive or the result of a redecorating project, you don't have to wait for the perfect scene. So many people will create their ideal writing space only to never set foot in it, never write a word, and it just adds to the list of reasons you can tell yourself that you are not a real writer. Write anywhere, just be comfortable while you are doing it. It may help to get out of the house and sit in a coffee shop. Sometimes that noise around us can deaden the silence of the white page. Local libraries have tables and study areas, parks have tables, and cars are somewhere to sit. Don't limit yourself, spread your wings and write. The minimum you need is somewhere to sit (the floor), something to lean on (your knee), a pen and some paper. It never has to be complicated and the simpler you keep it, the fewer excuses you will have for not getting it done.

- Set achievable goals for your writing, such as daily word counts or completing a chapter within a specific time frame. I would say I will write a minimum of one thousand words, five times a week, as opposed to a thousand words daily. Let's do the maths— one thousand words for five days a week, equals fifty thousand words in ten weeks, sixty thousand words in twelve weeks, and you get the picture. See how you can grow your novel? Your book? Your magnum opus?

- Keep a journal or idea notebook to jot down inspiration, thoughts and observations throughout the day.

- Read widely within your genre and outside of it to expose yourself to different writing styles and techniques.

- Take part in writing workshops, conferences or retreats to learn from experienced authors and connect with other writers.

- Find a writing buddy or join a writing group for accountability, support and constructive feedback.

- Embrace the power of drafting and revision; don't expect perfection in your first draft.

- Experiment with different writing exercises and prompts to challenge yourself and spark new ideas.

- Take breaks when needed to avoid burnout, but always return to your writing.

- Celebrate your writing achievements, no matter how small, to maintain motivation and a positive outlook.

- Learn to accept constructive criticism and use it to grow as a writer.

- Develop a thick skin and don't let rejection or negative feedback discourage you from pursuing your writing goals.

- Continuously educate yourself about the craft of writing through books, articles and online resources.

- Maintain a healthy lifestyle, including regular exercise, a balanced diet and sufficient sleep, to support your creative energy.

- Disconnect from digital distractions when writing to maintain focus and productivity.

- Don't compare your writing journey to others; focus on your own progress and growth.

- Be open to exploring different genres, styles and formats to find what resonates with you.

- Seek inspiration from various sources, such as nature, art, music or personal experiences.

- Remember that consistency is key; small, regular efforts will lead to significant progress over time.

FREEWRITING

'Freewriting is the easiest way to get words on paper and the best all round practice in writing I know.'

Peter Elbow

I open my book to a new page. I look around. It doesn't matter where I am. If I am home, in a cafe, a library, school, a park. I scan my surroundings and pick the first things my eyes land on. Today, I can see:

- *A karate class going on.*

- *Two mums are talking.*

- *The bored nine-year-old sister of one of the boys training is cracking her knuckles.*

It took me no time at all to find three things. If I sit here longer, I could list more, but I will resign myself to writing about each topic for ten minutes in turn. I want to see where they will lead me. I have an hour left of sitting here while my husband teaches class. My role as administrator is done for the day and today is not my training day. So I will write.

I put the title at the top of my first page—I write 'Karate Class' and away I go, for the next ten minutes. Where does it lead me? It doesn't matter. It is a lesson in observation, in writing about the things I see, naming what is in front of me, practising finding the words quickly.

I never know where a topic will lead me. I just go with it. When we are on the edge of discomfort, when we are about to unwrap that truth hidden in all of us, don't let go. Write and keep writing. This is our notebook. What we choose to share with the world is up to us.

Dig deep, that is where the gold is, that is where we find the grit and truth that so many of our favourite writers know how to unpack. It doesn't matter whether you write fiction or non-fiction, you need to get down to the grit of it!

Sometimes when you are writing, you can feel it in the pit of your stomach. There is a sense of dread. You are entering a room you would rather not be in. Don't shy away, shoulders back, deep breath and keep your hand moving, keep writing, bring it all up. You can decide what to do with it later.

It is so important that you release it all, that you get down to the depths of all that you may have previously been unable to say, to face, to relinquish. This is not therapy as such, but you can't be expected to create new and wonderful writing when your closets are filled to bursting. Where will the new ideas grow?

I often treat my main characters appallingly. I throw things at them I would never wish on my worst enemy.

Where it comes from, I don't know, but it is there, as is the strength to survive such terrible happenings. I let people's random and flippant comments in the past stop me from writing, cause me to hide or write and then disregard. How wonderful it was when I got my first computer and realised I could put a password on my writing so there would be no more misunderstandings. I didn't want anyone to think badly of me, think I was crazy or a potential psychopath. I am not. I am really a nice person. I hate violence, I hate abuse, I hate meanness and betrayal, but that doesn't mean that I don't want to write about it.

I was in a workshop recently with Holly Rigland, author of *The House That Joy Built*, and she talked about her other book *The Flowers*. It was the story that she had to write to allow other stories to come through. And that in a nutshell is the reality of being a writer: you can't be afraid to include everything you know, feel or wonder about the human condition. It is what keeps us showing up in our lives every day. We are all battling the human condition; we are shaped by our experiences, good or bad, and as authors we must use what we have felt, seen, heard and survived. Don't let the tribulations of your life be discarded. It all means something. It can all be used.

Don't hold back when you are writing. The time to be discerning is choosing what you share. Don't let your mother-in-law read about how awful you think she is. How you are sick of her cooking, think she wears too much perfume and needs to stop babying your fifty-year-old husband. But build her character, use her disguised in a book, spread her traits out through several characters and have them all get hit by cars in tragic accidents, but don't miss the opportunity to get it all off your chest.

•

Writing
Exercise

Look around you—pick the first three things you see. Even if you can't think of anything else to say, write about that. Write—*this is stupid, I don't know what to write, my dad was right when he said I should aim to get a proper job, I could never be a writer ...*

Don't give up if you feel the well is running dry, rewrite your topic and go again.

USING PROMPTS

'You can't wait for inspiration.
You have to go after it with a club.'

Jack London

In my workshops, I guide my students to write for ten minutes on a prompt. These are designed to open up the writer's mind and allow creative energy to flow. I am always surprised where these simple prompts can take us.

I aim to write every day, but it has taken me many years to get to the stage of my life where I honour writing as a regular daily practice. Not that I stick to writing every day, but I aim to, and I do not beat myself up if I miss a day or two.

I carry my notebook everywhere, and a collection of pens. I find moments wherever possible. I don't make a big song and dance about it, I don't have to be in the mood, in a special place or for the weather to be just right and the sky a selective shade of blue! Just write, that is what I do. This is in a notebook with a pen, a fountain pen if I am home and a Bic four-colour pen if I am out and about. The point is—don't make it difficult, don't make it a big deal. This is part of you. Writing is who you are and you need to embrace it into every facet of your daily life.

Rules for Writing Practice

- Keep your hand moving.

- Don't cross out, don't worry about grammar or spelling, just keep going knowing everything can be fixed later.

- Remember this writing is for you, you alone, you might feel confronted, get scared and nervous. You may even cry. All of that is fine. You are getting deeper into your mind.

- Don't get hung up on details but add in as much original detail as comes.

- Do not censor yourself. Go where the work leads you.

- If you get stuck, rewrite the prompt and keep going.

Below are some prompts I like to use. Some were inspired by Natalie Goldberg; others have come to be through writing practice. You will discover as you continue this practice and reread your work, some things will stand out to you and beckon you to dig deeper, to explore the topic further. When you find these gems, underline them and write them in the back of your notebook. Use this list to kick off another timed writing session.

Writing prompts

- I remember
- I was thinking about
- The first thing I remember
- I wish that I could have
- I never understood
- I want you to understand
- What happens when I die
- What would happen if I just walked away
- Maybe I wasn't born here
- Everything I love
- I don't like
- A teacher I admire
- A teacher who underestimated me
- Who made me feel foolish
- Who loves me
- Who do I love
- Who would I say sorry to
- A holiday
- A celebration
- A missed celebration
- Talk about regrets

- An animal
- Talk about learning something new
- Cooking a favourite meal
- What did I eat, and enjoy
- What don't I like the taste of
- What do I see when I look up
- What do I see when I look down
- A place I want to go
- A night I cannot sleep
- The things I carry
- What can I put down
- A car trip
- A train trip
- A bus
- A boat
- Staying in a hotel
- Eating out
- A walk
- A run
- A present
- Red (don't use the word red)
- Blue (don't use the word blue)

- Black

- White

- Something I lost

- Something I found

- Favourite toy

- Learning to drive

- Hot

- Cold

- Autumn

- Spring

- Water

- Fire

- Kindness

- Cruelty

- Happy

- Anger

- Worry

- Fishing

- Sport

- Sunday

- Monday

- Nighttime

- Daytime

- Out to lunch

- Rainbow

- Weather

- Worry

- Kiss

- The last time

- A first time

- Dancing

- Running

- What made you sing?

- Animal

- Peaceful

- Chaos

- Friendship

- Love

- Broken hearted

- Surprise

- Disappointment

- Discovery

- I said

- I heard

Writing
Exercise

Try sprints: when you only have a few minutes, use one of the above prompts and write for three minutes or half a page.

VISUAL ART AS A
WRITING PROMPT

'A photograph is a secret about a secret.
The more it tells you the less you know.'

Diane Arbus

While a photograph might seem to reveal everything at first glance, there's always more beneath the surface—the emotions, the context, the untold stories. A picture is worth a thousand words, as the saying goes. How can a picture inspire you? Have you ever looked out over a vista and wanted to write, to draw, to capture the image on your phone, to remember?

Look at a photo on your phone now. Think about everything in that moment.

- Where are you? Describe the place, the smell, the feel. Was it hot or cold, did you bring a cardigan?

- Who is with you, friend or foe?

- Did you eat? Was it nice, was it terrible?

- What did you talk about?

- Describe the decor.

- Did you drink anything?

- Did you make eyes across the room?

- Did someone make you annoyed?

- Did you see someone else making eyes?

- Describe the scene.

- Morning or night?

- How does the air smell?

- Who is there?

- What could happen here?

Writing

Exercise

Practise with random pictures you find. Check out the internet, Facebook, Pinterest, magazines, newspapers. Describe everything you see and everything that is implied.

DRAWING

Have you tried drawing a scene? Perhaps you are artistic or maybe you aren't well practised, you don't think that you can draw, and that it is something better left to the experts. Try it. Put your pen to paper and draw the scene in front of you now.

Below is a drawing of my desk – as you can see I am not a great artist, but you get the idea.

Draw the scene well enough so that you can recognise what is in front of you. Try not to stick just to stick figures but flesh out the objects, people, animals and fauna in your scene. Don't judge, keep going. This drawing is between you and the page.

Drawing a scene will train your eyes to see the finer details, perhaps pick up the texture of the cloth of his shirt, the silkiness of the leaves on the elephant plant, the prickly thorns on the rose and the dew on the petals. It opens your eyes to the finer details, and it is these details, that will bring your writing to life.

A student of mine recently said that she drew well enough to get her point across. That's it. That is all you have to do. Draw a scene well enough to know what you are looking at. Don't make this hard. Use your notebook and pen to draw. You don't have to have an easel and a professional paint palette.

Writing
Exercise

Draw something that is right in front of you.

SKETCH WITH WORDS

'The writer should never be ashamed of staring.
There is nothing that does not require his attention.'

Flannery O'Connor

This is a great exercise to do when you are short of time or ideas. Just like an artist would sketch a scene with a pencil, take out your pen and sketch a scene with words until you come up with something that can be 'coloured' in later.

Example: to my left is a window outside, a little five-shelf timber spice rack I use to store my essential oils. Next to that is a little square timber and white painted bathroom caddy shelf I use for storing art supplies— watercolour pencils, paintbrushes, gauche paints, tissues, a book about the orphanage in Adelaide I haven't read yet. Spare glasses, my neck brace, compass set I bought in an op shop in Victor Harbour because I liked that the box it came in locked and unlocked by pulling a nail in and out. On my desk is a box of photos and mail, a red cup with a typewriter on it containing an assortment of writing pens, a letter opener and some paintbrushes …

I could go on, I haven't even made it to the working part of my office yet.

Writing
Exercise

Pick a scene. It can be a place you are, one you have visited or a photograph. Use your words as you would the lines of a pencil. Draw your image with words. Put in as much detail as you can, time yourself for fifteen minutes. Go!

BE INSPIRED
BY ART

'Every artist dips his brush in his own soul,
and paints his own nature into his pictures.'

Henry Ward Beecher

Art has long been a wellspring of inspiration, offering a visual feast that can spark creativity, evoke emotions, and birth new narratives. The interplay between visual arts and literature is a dance as old as human expression itself, with each medium enriching and informing the other.

Paintings, sculptures, and other visual artworks often tell stories without words. These silent narratives can be a jumping-off point for expansive tales. A portrait might inspire a character study, while a landscape could set the scene for an epic adventure. We become an interpreter, translating brush strokes and colour palettes into vivid prose.

Art has an unparalleled ability to evoke emotions, and writers can tap into this wellspring of feeling. An abstract expressionist piece might convey a sense of chaos or jubilation that a writer can channel into their work. The melancholy of a Picasso blue period painting could infuse a poem with palpable sorrow.

By immersing ourselves in art, we can access and articulate complex emotions that might otherwise remain elusive. The visual becomes a bridge to the visceral, allowing us to convey feelings with greater depth and authenticity.

Writing
Exercise

1. *Choose an image: select a photograph, painting or any visual that captures your interest.*

2. *Observe carefully: study the image. Notice colours, shapes, objects, people and the overall mood.*

3. *Ask questions: generate questions about the image. Who are the people? What's happening? What led to this moment?*

4. *Use sensory details: imagine what you might hear, smell, taste or feel if you were in the scene.*

5. *Create a story: develop a narrative based on the image. It could be about what's happening in the picture, what led to this moment or what might happen next.*

6. *Describe the setting: use the visual details to create a vivid setting in your prose.*

7. *Develop characters: use their appearance and expressions to inspire character development.*

8. *Explore emotions: consider the emotions evoked by the image and incorporate them into your writing.*

9. *Write freely: start writing without overthinking. Let the image guide your prose.*

10. *Revise and refine: after your initial draft, revise your work to enhance the connection between the image and your prose.*

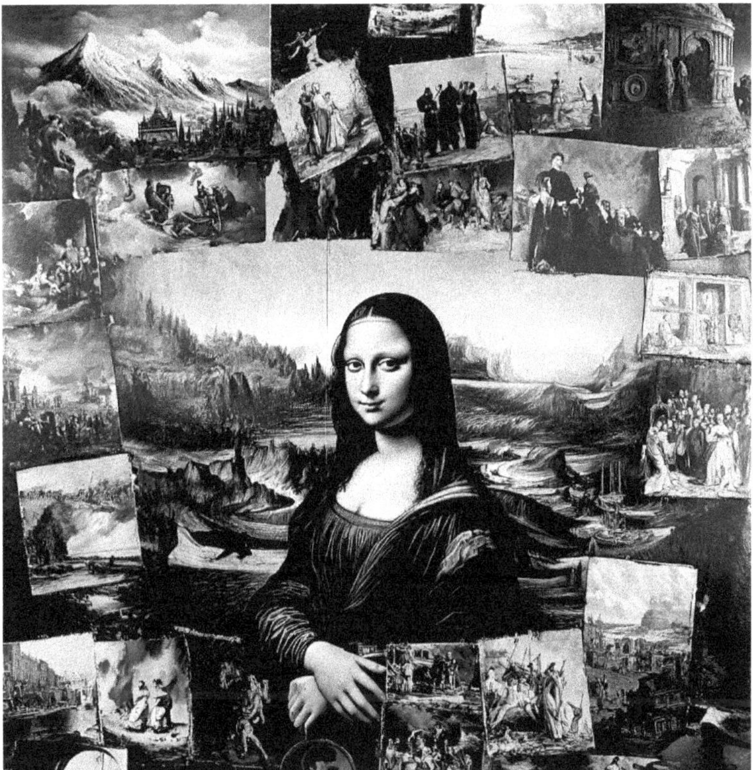

WORDPLAY

Wordplay is a powerful tool that can enhance creativity, improve linguistic skills and add depth to our work. It encourages us to think outside the box and challenges us to find new and unexpected connections between words and ideas.

Regular engagement with word play naturally expands our vocabulary. As we search for the perfect word to complete a pun or craft a clever alliteration, we often discover new words or rediscover forgotten ones. This expanded lexicon provides us with a richer palette from which to paint our literary pictures.

Moreover, word play deepens our understanding of language structures and rules. To successfully bend or break these rules for effect, we must first thoroughly understand them. This enhanced linguistic awareness can lead to more precise and effective writing overall.

I've created a word chain starting with PEN and ending with NOVEL, using sixty words in total. Each word is associated with the one before and after it, creating a flow of ideas related to writing and storytelling.

PEN → INK → STAIN → MARK → IMPRESSION → IMPACT → FORCE → POWER → STRENGTH → CHARACTER → PROTAGONIST → HERO → JOURNEY → ADVENTURE → STORY → PLOT → TWIST → TURN → PAGE → BOOK → LIBRARY → KNOWLEDGE → WISDOM → SAGE → MENTOR → GUIDE → PATH → QUEST → CHALLENGE → CONFLICT → RESOLUTION → ENDING → CLOSURE → SATISFACTION → READER → AUDIENCE → RECEPTION → CRITIQUE → REVIEW → REFLECTION → MIRROR → IMAGE → DESCRIPTION → DETAIL → NUANCE → SUBTLETY → CRAFT → ART → EXPRESSION → VOICE → ECHO → RESONANCE → THEME → MOTIF → PATTERN → STRUCTURE → FRAMEWORK → OUTLINE → DRAFT → REVISION → POLISH → SHINE → BRILLIANCE → GENIUS → AUTHOR → CREATOR → IMAGINATION → FANTASY → REALM → WORLD-BUILDING → SETTING → SCENE → ACTION → DIALOGUE → CONVERSATION → EXCHANGE → INTERACTION → DYNAMIC → TENSION → SUSPENSE → ANTICIPATION → CLIMAX → PINNACLE → ACHIEVEMENT → MASTERPIECE → NOVEL

This type of wordplay can be useful for:

1. Brainstorming: it can help generate new ideas or connections you might not have thought of otherwise.

2. Vocabulary building: it encourages you to think of related words, potentially expanding your vocabulary.

3. Creative exercise: it can serve as a warm-up activity to get your creative juices flowing before a writing session.

4. Story prompts: you could use sections of the chain or the entire chain as inspiration for a story or poem.

5. Understanding connections: it illustrates how different aspects of writing and storytelling are interconnected.

Writing
Exercise

Create your own word chain.

Some suggestions:

- Whimsical

- Labyrinth

- Harmony

- Yodel

- Lullaby

- Yacht

- Thesaurus

- Serendipity

- Yarn

- Nostalgia

- Aroma

- Aesthetic

- Charisma

- Allure

- Eloquent

- Tranquil

- Luminous

- Serenity

- Youthful

- Laughter

- Romance

- Fighting

- Death

- Marriage

- Family

- Universe

- Politics

- Royalty

- Emotions

- Silence

- Celebration

- Travel

MIND MAPPING

To create a mind map for your writing project, start by placing your main idea or story concept in the centre of a blank page. Draw a circle around it. From this central idea, branch out with lines to represent major themes, characters, or plot points. Write these key elements at the end of each line.

For each of these branches, create sub-branches to explore related ideas, details or possibilities. Use different colours for various categories or levels of information to make your map visually engaging and easy to navigate.

Don't censor your ideas; let your thoughts flow freely, adding branches and sub-branches as new connections emerge.

Include symbols, sketches or small illustrations to represent concepts visually. If you hit a dead end on one branch, simply move to another—the beauty of mind mapping is its flexibility.

As your map grows, look for unexpected connections between different branches, which can lead to unique plot twists or character developments. Remember, there's no right or wrong way to mind map; the goal is to stimulate your creativity and organise your thoughts in a way that makes sense to you. Once your mind map feels complete, use it as a reference to guide your writing process, but don't be afraid to deviate from it if your story takes an unexpected turn. Your mind map is a tool for inspiration, not a rigid outline.

Below is a photo of the mind map I created in my notebook when I was planning this book…

Writing
Exercise

Think of your next writing product and start formulating your mind map.

ACRONYM
EXPANSION

Take a word related to your chosen topic and use each letter as the start of a new word or phrase, creating a branching effect.

Example:

WRITE: words, reveal, ideas, through, expression

NOVEL: narrative, of, vivid, engaging, literature

EDIT: enhance, develop, improve, transform

STORY: sequence, that, orchestrates, riveting, yarns

PLOT: purposeful, linking, of, turning points

CHARACTER: complex, human, attributes, rendered, artfully, compelling, tales, everywhere, resonating

DRAFT: developing, raw, artistic, framework, thoroughly

REVISE: refine, evaluate, verify, improve, strengthen, enhance

PROSE: powerful, rhythmic, orchestration, sentences, expression

AUTHOR: architect, unique, tales, harmonising, original, reflections

Word-related acronym exercises, can be useful for:

- Creativity boosts: these exercises challenge you to think creatively, finding words that fit both the letter constraint and the overall theme.

- Vocabulary enhancement: as you search for words to fit each letter, you often encounter or remember words you don't use frequently, thus expanding your active vocabulary.

- Mnemonic devices: acronyms can serve as memory aids. For instance, 'WRITE' expanded to 'Words Reveal Ideas Through Expression' can help you remember the essence of writing.

- Brainstorming: when stuck on a writing project, creating acronyms related to your topic can spark new ideas or perspectives.

- Word association skills: it improves your ability to make quick associations between words and concepts, which is valuable in various forms of writing.

- Linguistic play: encourage playfulness with language, which can lead to more engaging and creative writing.

- Focus on key concepts: by distilling a concept into an acronym, you're forced to consider its most important aspects.

- Ice-breakers: in writing groups or classes, these can serve as fun ice-breakers or warm-up exercises.

Writing
Exercise

Create your own lists around food, your house, your family and friends, your job, your books…

ALLITERATION EXERCISES

Create phrases or sentences where every word starts with the same letter, encouraging lateral thinking.

A: ambitious authors artfully arrange alluring adventures.

B: brave bards breathe boundless beauty into bustling books.

C: clever characters cleverly craft captivating conclusions.

Writing
Exercise

Create your own alliterative phrases or sentences related to a specific genre or aspect of writing—mystery, romance, character development, plot twists.

YOUR WRITING
TOOLS

Equipment-wise, writing is one of the simplest activities to prepare for. There are only three things you need to begin:

- Your mind

- Your pen

- Your notebook

Everything else is a bonus.

Computer – desktop or laptop. If you don't have one, you can book sessions at the library to use their computers for free.

Printer – again if you don't have one you have one you can get documents printed at the library or places like Officeworks for a small fee.

Software for Writers

Here's a list of writing software that can enhance your productivity and creativity, categorised into paid and free options:

Paid Software $$

1. Scrivener ($49 for standard license)

   ▶ Comprehensive writing studio

   ▶ Excellent for long-form writing and organising research

   ▶ Available for Windows, Mac and iOS

2. Final Draft ($249.99)

   ▶ Industry standard for screenwriting

   ▶ Formatting tools specific to film and TV scripts

   ▶ Available for Windows and Mac

3. Ulysses ($5.99/month or $49.99/year)

   ▶ Clean, distraction-free writing environment

   ▶ Markdown-based text editor

   ▶ Available for Mac and iOS only

4. ProWritingAid ($20/month, $79/year or $399 lifetime)

    ► Advanced grammar and style checker

    ► Detailed reports on writing style

    ► Available as a web app and desktop software

5. Plottr ($25/year or $65 lifetime)

    ► Visual plot outlining and timeline creation

    ► Character development tools

    ► Available for Windows, Mac and mobile devices

Free Software (with some paid features)

1. Grammarly

    ► Grammar and spell checker

    ► Basic version is free, premium features available

    ► Works across multiple platforms

2. Hemingway Editor

    ► Helps improve readability and conciseness

    ► Free web version, paid desktop app ($19.99)

3. Evernote

    ▶ Note-taking and organisation tool

    ▶ Basic version is free, premium features available

    ▶ Cross-platform synchronisation

4. Notion

    ▶ All-in-one workspace for notes, tasks and databases

    ▶ Generous free plan, team plans available

    ▶ Available on web, desktop and mobile

5. Google Docs

    ▶ Cloud-based word processor

    ▶ Completely free with a Google account

    ▶ Excellent for collaboration

Completely Free Software

1. yWriter

    ▶ Novel-writing program

    ▶ Helps organise chapters and scenes

    ▶ Available for Windows and Linux

2. Focus Writer

   ▸ Distraction-free writing environment

   ▸ Customisable backgrounds and themes

   ▸ Available for Windows, Mac and Linux

3. LibreOffice Writer

   ▸ Full-featured word processor

   ▸ Compatible with Microsoft Word files

   ▸ Available for Windows, Mac and Linux

4. Reedsy Book Editor

   ▸ Free online writing and formatting tool

   ▸ Designed for creating print-ready book files

   ▸ Works in any web browser

5. Bibisco

   ▸ Novel-writing software with character development tools

   ▸ Basic version is free, paid version available

   ▸ Available for Windows, Mac and Linux

Remember, the best software for you depends on your specific needs, writing style and the type of projects you're working on. Many of these tools offer free trials, so you can test them before committing to a purchase.

THE TOOLKIT WRITING DECK

Each table on the following pages represents a category. Copy and cut these out, colour the back of each category or mark in a way that it remains distinguishable. At the beginning of your writing practice, choose one topic from each category. In your writing session use each of the details you have selected.

Winter	Fire	Autumn
Spring	Wet	Flood
Summer	Storm	Dry

I was thinking of	I remember	Once upon a time...
I don't remember	I don't know	I wasn't thinking of
I know	I have something to tell you	I didn't want to tell you

Jealous	Sad	Relax
Disappoinment	Angry	Painful
Confusion	Regret	Happy

Someone with power	Woman	Man
Child	Stranger	Teacher
Someone disempowered	Work colleague	Friend

Black	White	Green
Yellow	Clear	Orange
Red	Blue	Grey

Running	Playing sport	Roller skating
Driving	Hiking	Sex
Walking	Cycling	Dancing

Where you slept	Where you said goodbye	A place in nature you know
Where you will die	Where you grew up	A place of interest you have seen
Where you said hello	A town or city you know	A familiar routine

THE LAST WORD

As we come to the end of this book, I hope you've found a spark—or perhaps rekindled a flame—that will keep you writing long after you've turned the last page. Remember, the journey of a writer is not a straight path but a winding road filled with unexpected turns, breathtaking vistas, and yes, sometimes a few bumps along the way.

Throughout these pages, we've explored the nooks and crannies of the writing life. We've delved into the 'why' of writing, confronted the demons of self-doubt, and armed ourselves with tools to silence that ever-critical inner editor. We've learned to embrace our monkey minds, turning what could be a distraction into a wellspring of creativity.

But more than anything, I hope you've realised that being a writer isn't about publishing bestsellers or winning literary awards—though those things are nice, of course. It's about regularly showing up to the page and putting your heart down in words. It's about observing the world around you with the keen eye of a storyteller, finding inspiration in the mundane and magic in the everyday.

Remember, your writing practice is uniquely yours. Whether you're scribbling in notebooks during your lunch break, tapping away on your laptop in the wee hours of the morning, or dictating stories into your phone while stuck in traffic, you're a writer. Embrace it. Own it. Celebrate it.

Don't let anyone—least of all yourself—tell you that your words don't matter. They do. Every time you put pen to paper or fingers to keyboard, you're creating something that didn't exist before. You're adding your voice to the grand tapestry of human expression. And that, my fellow writer, is a beautiful thing.

So, what now? Well, now you write. You take all the prompts, exercises, and insights from this book and you run with them. You fill notebooks, hard drives, and the margins of newspapers with your words. You experiment, you play, you fail, and you try again. You nurture your creative self with artist dates and tend to your physical well-being with desk yoga and mindful breaks.

Most importantly, you keep going. On the days when the words flow like a river and on the days when each syllable feels like it's being extracted with pliers. You write because you're a writer, and that's what writers do.

Remember, I'm rooting for you. Every time you sit down to write, imagine me—and countless other writers around the world—cheering you on. We're all in this together, each of us trying to make sense of the world one word at a time.

So, go forth and write. Fill the world with your stories, your insights, your unique perspective. Be brave, be persistent, and above all, be you. Your words are waiting. Your readers are waiting.

What are you waiting for? Close this book, open your notebook, and write.

'One of the few things I know about writing is this: spend it all, shoot it, play it, lose it, all, right away, every time. Do not hoard what seems good for a later place in the book, or for another book; give it, give it all, give it now ... something more will arise for later, something better. These things fill you from behind, from beneath, like well water. Similarly, the impulse to keep to yourself what you have learned is not only shameful, it is destructive. Anything you do not give freely and abundantly becomes lost to you. You open your safe and find ashes.'

Annie Dillard

WEEKLY SCHEDULE TEMPLATE

'Writers write. Everyone else makes excuses.'

Jack Bickham

Book in your writing time now and keep the appointment with your writing self.

	Monday	Tuesday	Wednesday	Thursday	Friday	Saturday	Sunday
5 a.m.							
6 a.m.							
7 a.m.							
8 a.m.							
9 a.m.							
10 a.m.							
11 a.m.							
12 p.m.							
1 p.m.							
2 p.m.							
3 p.m.							
4 p.m.							
5 p.m.							
6 p.m.							
7 p.m.							
8 p.m.							
9 p.m.							
10 p.m.							
11 p.m.							
12 a.m.							
1 a.m.							
2 a.m.							
3 a.m.							
4 a.m.							

ACKNOWLEDGEMENTS

This book would not be possible without the influence of every author I have read, every writer I have met, every teacher I have had, and every author podcast I have listened to.

Special thanks to Joanna Penn from the *Creative Penn Podcast* for leading the way for Indie Authors.

Sincerest thanks to Natalie Goldberg whose books, talks, art and workshops are a gift of love, truth and wisdom, and have been a major influence on my writing life.

BIBLIOGRAPHY

Atwood, Margaret (2002) *On Writers and Writing.* Virago Press.

Bell, James Scott (2009) *The Art of War for Writers.* Writer's Digest Books.

Cameron, Julia (2020) *The Artist's Way.* Penguin Random House.

Cameron, Julie, Goldberg Natalie (2015) *The Writing Life.* Sounds True.

Dillard, Annie (1990) *The Writing Life.* Harper and Rowe.

Gemmell, Nikki (2019) *On Quiet.* Bolinda Audio.

Gemmell, Nikki (2021) *Dissolve.* Hachette Australia.

Gilbert, Elizabeth (2015) *Big Magic.* Riverhead Books.

Goldberg, Natalie (1999) *Wild Mind.* Writer's Audio Shop.

Goldberg, Natalie (2014) *The True Secret of Writing.* Simon & Schuster.

Goldberg, Natalie (1986) *Writing Done the Bones.* Shambala Publications.

Herring, Laraine (2007) *Writing Begins With the Breath.* Shambhala Trade.

Keyes, Ralph (1995) *The Courage to Write.* Henry Holt Publications.

King, Stephen (2012) *On Writing: A Memoir of the Craft.* Hodder Publications.

Lamott, Anne (1994) *Bird by Bird*. Scribe Publications.

Nestor, James (2021) *Breath: The New Science of a Lost Art.* Penguin Like.

Penn, Joanna (2023) *Writing the Shadow*. Curl Up Press.

Syme, Becca (2021) *Dear Writer, You're Doing it Right*. Hummingbird Books.

Zinsser, William (2019) *On Writing Well*. Harper Collins.

www.ingramcontent.com/pod-product-compliance
Lightning Source LLC
Chambersburg PA
CBHW052011030426
42334CB00029BA/3179